Ron Paul
vs.
Barack Obama
On The Issues

**Jesse Gordon,
OnTheIssues.org**

Table of Contents

Paul vs. Obama on International Issues..............107

Book reviews 141

Paul vs. Obama on VoteMatch:.........................156

Paul vs. Obama On The Issues

Representative Ron Paul of Texas and President Barack Obama agree on some issues and disagree on many others. This book outlines their stances on the issues, in a side-by-side manner for each issue, on many of the controversial topics that they will face as President.

We gather the two candidates' issue stances from their political autobiographies; from debates in both the 2012 election season and past elections; from public speeches; from campaign websites; and from political analysis websites. All of the excerpts appear, with many additional issue stances, on our website, www.OnTheIssues.org.

Obama is unopposed for the 2012 Democratic nomination, so we focus on his presidential speeches, as well as materials from past campaigns. Paul is most famous for inspiring the online revolution which initiated the Tea Party movement. This book explores the issues underlying both of these candidates' past victories.

The purpose of this book, and the mission of our website, is to inform voters about candidates' issue stances—what they believe about the issues, and what they have done to implement those beliefs. The mainstream media report on candidates' politics: who's ahead this week; who "won" the last debate; who has endorsed whom. We reject the "horse race politics" that dominates the mainstream media, and instead focus on what matters: Paul on the issues versus Obama on the issues.

—Jesse Gordon, Editor-in-Chief, jesse@OnTheIssues.org
January 2012

Dedication

To Lewis & Ram

Acknowledgments

This book would not have been possible without the tireless efforts of the entire OnTheIssues team: Derek Camara, Janice Gordon, Michele Gordon, Peter Hoerr, Ram Lau, Adam Leighton, Jamie Leighton, Naomi Lichtenberg, Ogden Porter, Will Rico, Dan Teittinen, Irma Teittinen, and especially Kathleen Camara.

Paul vs. Obama
on Domestic Issues

Domestic issues focus on joint state-federal jurisdiction or enforcement, including the following topics:

- *Crime:* including mandatory sentencing and the death penalty. Rep. Paul opposes both on libertarian grounds; President Obama opposes both on liberal grounds.

- *Gun Control:* Rep Paul focuses on the individual right as opposed to Pres. Obama's "collective right" to gun ownership, which allows local restrictions.

- *Drugs:* including marijuana legalization and the War on Drugs. Paul's libertarian hands-off policy compares with Obama's hands-off attitude towards the topic of legalization.

- *Environment:* including pollution and EPA issues. Obama demonstrates a progressive attitude of enforcing anti-pollution and pro-animal-rights policies, and hence is more the environmentalist than Paul's property rights-based approach. Their differences converge on opposing Yucca Mountain nuclear waste storage.

- *Technology and Infrastructure:* including high-tech Internet and privacy issues, as well as low-tech roads and bridges investment issues. Obama and Paul agree on issues of privacy and limiting investments in outer space, but disagree on "Net Neutrality."

- *Health Care:* including federal healthcare and ObamaCare issues; plus Medicare/Medicaid and state issues. The two candidates disagree on the central issue of ObamaCare, but Paul is not a hard-core repealist on the subject.

Ron Paul
on Domestic Issues

Barack Obama
on Domestic Issues

Paul on Hate Crime

Replace "hate crime" with equal penalties
for equal assaults

The idea that a crime can be judged as to whether it was motivated by hate for certain groups introduces the notion of a thought police. It implies that some victims have greater worth than others. The extra and arbitrary enforcement power mocks the principle of equal justice before the law.

Why should the penalty for assault be different depending on the race, sexual orientation or membership in a particular group? Because some criminals have in the past been punished less harshly due to their victim's belonging to a particular group is hardly a justification for a criminal to be punished more harshly for the same reason.

It's best we drop the whole concept of hyphenated rights and refer only to individual rights. When hate crime legislation is written or proposed it comes up short in promoting justice. Hate crime legislation and the obsession with political correctness seem to satisfy the urge to condemn thoughtless people by misusing the law.

Source: Liberty Defined, by Rep. Ron Paul, p.148-149, April 19, 2011

Obama on Hate Crime

Lack of enforcement sets tone for more hate crimes

OBAMA: [to Biden]: There is a consequence to the demagoguery [over immigration]—hate crimes against Latinos have gone way up over the last year. We've also seen over the last several months this epidemic of nooses being hung all across the country since the events down in Jena, Louisiana. And it indicates the degree to which a president has to set a tone of bringing all people together as opposed to excluding people. And being willing to talk about racial issues when they arise and having a civil rights division of the justice department that is aggressive about investigating. So, what can we do to strengthen the enforcement of hate crimes legislation? It is something that I will prioritize as president but I don't want to have to wait until I am.

BIDEN: We can and we should move [the pending Hate Crimes legislation] forward. The impediment right now is the president. I would not wait.

Source: Iowa Brown & Black Presidential Forum, Dec. 1, 2007

Pass ENDA and expand hate crime legislation

We must be careful to keep our eyes on the prize—equal rights for every American. We must continue to fight for the Employment Non Discrimination Act. We must expand hate crime legislation and be vigilant about how these laws are enforced—.continue to expand adoption rights to make them consistent—and we must repeal the "Don't ask, don't tell' military policy.

Source: In His Own Words, edited by Lisa Rogak, p. 44, March 27, 2007

Paul on Alternative Sentencing

Voted YES on funding for alternative sentencing instead of more prisons

Vote on an amendment that would reduce the funding for violent offender imprisonment by and truth-in-sentencing programs by $61 million. The measure would increase funding for Boys and Girls Clubs and drug courts by the same amount.

Source: Amendment sponsored by Scott, D-VA; Bill HR 4690;
vote number 317 on June 22, 2000

Voted NO on more prosecution and sentencing for juvenile crime

Vote to pass a bill to appropriate $1.5 billion to all of the states that want to improve their juvenile justice operations. Among other provisions this bill includes funding for development, implementation, and administration of graduated sanctions for juvenile offenders, funds for building, expanding, or renovating juvenile corrections facilities, hiring juvenile judges, probation officers, and additional prosecutors for juvenile cases.

Source: Bill introduced by McCollum, R-FL; Bill HR 1501;
vote number 233 on June 17, 1999

Obama on Alternative Sentencing

Supports alternative sentencing and rehabilitation

Principles that Obama supports to address crime:

- Implement penalties other than incarceration for certain non-violent offenders.

- Increase state funds for programs which rehabilitate and educate inmates during and after their prison sentences.

- Provide funding for military-style "boot camps" for first-time juvenile felons.

Source: State Legislative National Political Awareness Test, July 2, 1998

Reduce recidivism by giving offenders a Second Chance

Obama co-sponsored the Recidivism Reduction and Second Chance Act, which expands provisions for adult and juvenile offender state and local reentry demonstration projects. Directs the Attorney General to award grants for:

- State and local reentry courts;

- Comprehensive and Continuous Offender Reentry Task Forces;

- Drug treatment services to incarcerated offenders;

- Mentoring services for reintegrating offenders into the community;

- prison-based family treatment programs for incarcerated parents of minor children; and

Source: Second Chance Act (S.1060/H.R.1593) 08-S1060 on March 29, 2007

Paul on Death Penalty

Too many capital convictions
have been proven errors

There was a time I simply stated that I supported the death penalty. Now my views are not so clearly defined. I do not support the federal death penalty, but constitutionally I cannot, as a federal official, interfere with the individual states that impose it. After years spent in Washington, I have become more aware than ever of the government's ineptness and the likelihood of its making mistakes.

I no longer trust the U.S. government to invoke and carry out a death sentence under any condition. Too many convictions, not necessarily federal, have been found to be in error, but only after years of incarcerating innocent people who later were released on DNA evidence. Rich people when guilty are rarely found guilty and sentenced to death. For me it's much easier just to eliminate the ultimate penalty and incarcerate the guilty for life—in case later evidence proves a mistaken conviction.

Source: Liberty Defined, by Rep. Ron Paul, p. 32-33, April 19, 2011

Obama on Death Penalty

Battled legislatively against the death penalty

Obama's most significant contribution has been his legislative battles against the death penalty, and against in the criminal justice system. In Illinois, it's been a series of shocking exonerations of innocent people who are on death row. He was involved very intimately in drafting and passing legislation that requires the video taping of police interrogations and confessions in all capital cases. And he also was one of the co-sponsors of this very comprehensive reform or the death penalty system in Illinois, which many people say may trigger the retreat on the death penalty in many other states.

Source: Salim Muwakkil and Amy Goodman, Democracy Now,
Jul 15, 2004

Death penalty should be enforced fairly and with caution

I think that the death penalty is appropriate in certain circumstances. There are especially heinous crimes: terrorism, the harm of children. Obviously, we've had some problems in this state in the application of the death penalty. That's why a moratorium was put in place and that's why I was so proud to be one of the leaders in overhauling a death penalty system that was broken. We became the first in the nation requiring the video taping of capital interrogations and confessions. We have to have this ultimate sanction in certain circumstances where the whole community says "this is beyond the pale."

Source: Illinois Senate Debate #3: Barack Obama vs. Alan Keyes,
Oct 21, 2004

Paul on Gun Rights

Opposes the DC Gun Ban;
it's not just a "collective right"

An appeals court in Washington DC issued a ruling that hopefully will result in the restoration of 2nd Amendment rights in the nation's capital. It appears the Court rejected the nonsensical argument that the 2nd Amendment confers only a "collective right," something gun control advocates have asserted for years. Rights, by definition, are individual. "Group rights" is an oxymoron.

When the 2nd Amendment speaks of a "well-regulated militia," it means local groups of individuals operating to protect their own families, homes, and communities. They regulated themselves because it was necessary and in their own interest to do so. The Founders themselves wrote in the Federalist papers about the need for individuals to be armed.

Gun control makes people demonstrably less safe—as any honest examination of criminal statistics reveals. It is no coincidence that violent crime flourishes in the nation's capital, where the individual's right to self-defense has been most severely curtailed.

Source: Weekly column, "Texas Straight Talk," March 12, 2007

Obama on Gun Rights

Respect 2nd Amendment, but local gun bans ok

Q: You said recently, "I have no intention of taking away folks' guns." How do you justify supporting the D.C. handgun ban?

A: Because I think we have two conflicting traditions in this country. I think it's important for us to recognize that we've got a tradition of handgun ownership and gun ownership generally. And a lot of law-abiding citizens use it for hunting, for sportsmanship, and for protecting their families. We also have a violence on the streets that is the result of illegal handgun usage. And so I think there is nothing wrong with a community saying we are going to take those illegal handguns off the streets. And cracking down on the various loopholes that exist in terms of background checks for children, the mentally ill. We can have reasonable gun control measure that I think respect the Second Amendment and people's traditions.

Source: 2008 Politico pre-Potomac Primary interview, Feb. 11, 2008

Provide some common-sense enforcement on gun licensing

Q: In the state senate, you talked about licensing and registering gun owners. Would you do that as president?

A: I don't think that we can get that done. But what we can do is to provide just some common-sense enforcement. The efforts by law enforcement to obtain the information required to trace back guns that have been used in crimes to unscrupulous gun dealers. As president, I intend to make it happen.

Source: 2008 Democratic debate in Las Vegas, Jan. 15, 2008

Paul on Drugs in Society

We don't need laws to tell us to not use heroin

Q: You say that the federal government should stay out of people's personal habits, including marijuana, cocaine, even heroin.

A: It's an issue of protecting liberty across the board. If you have the inconsistency, then you're really not defending liberty. We want freedom [including] when it comes to our personal habits.

Q: Are you suggesting that heroin and prostitution are an exercise of liberty?

A: Yes, in essence, if we leave it to the states. For over 100 years, they *were* legal. You're implying if we legalize heroin tomorrow, everyone's gonna use heroin.

How many people here are going to use heroin if it were legal? I bet nobody! "Oh yeah, I need the government to take care of me. I don't want to use heroin, so I need these laws!"

I never thought heroin would get applause!

Source: 2011 GOP primary debate in South Carolina, May 5, 2011

Obama on Drugs in Society

Expand drug courts; help prisoners with substance abuse

THE PROBLEM

Disparities Continue to Plague Criminal Justice System: African Americans and Hispanics are more than twice as likely as whites to be searched & arrested when stopped by police. Disparities in drug sentencing laws, like the differential treatment of crack as opposed to powder cocaine, are unfair.

OBAMA'S PLAN

- *Expand Use of Drug Courts:* Obama will give first-time, non-violent offenders a chance to serve their sentence, where appropriate, in the type of drug rehabilitation programs that have proven to work better than a prison term in changing bad behavior.

- *Reduce Crime Recidivism by Providing Ex-Offender Support:* Obama will provide job training, substance abuse and mental health counseling to ex-offenders, so that they are successfully re-integrated into society.

- *Eliminate Sentencing Disparities:* The disparity between sentencing crack and powder-based cocaine is wrong and should be completely eliminated.

Source: Campaign booklet, "Blueprint for Change," p. 49, Feb. 2, 2008

Paul on Marijuana Legalization

Legalize industrial hemp

Paul believes in the legalization of industrial hemp. Paul supported HR 3037 to amend the Controlled Substances Act to exclude industrial hemp from the definition of marijuana. This bill would have given the states the power to regulate farming of hemp. The measure would be a first since the national prohibition of industrial hemp farming in the United States. He favors the legalization of marijuana

Source: SourceWatch.org, Jan. 22, 2007

NOTE: Industrial hemp is a raw material commonly used for making paper, textiles, and other commercial products. In the United States, use of industrial hemp is banned because the plant is related to marijuana. Advocates of drug legalization push the issue of industrial hemp (and wear T-shorts made of industrial hemp) because it is a marginal issue that might gain support from moderates.

Obama on Marijuana Legalization

Not first candidate to use drugs, but first honest about it

One issue that exposed the disconnect between Obama's appeal & the conventional wisdom of an older generation is his drug use. The Washington Post focused on his use of drugs as a teen that he reveals in his book, Dreams from My Father: "Pot had helped, and booze; maybe a little blow when you could afford it. Not smack though."

Obama's honesty in addressing the issue reflects a generational change in politics. Most voters no longer care about youthful drug use; they're worried about having an honest person in the White House. In 1992, Bill Clinton answered a question about his drug use by saying he had tried marijuana, but "didn't inhale." When asked, "Did you inhale?" Obama replied, "That was the point." Obama was making fun of old-style politician who thought they could fool the voters.

Obama is almost certainly isn't the first person to use cocaine and then run for president. But he is the first presidential candidate honest enough to talk about the troubles of his youth.

Source: The Improbable Quest, by John K. Wilson, p. 12-13, Oct. 30, 2007

Paul on Nuclear Waste

No nuclear waste in Yucca Mountain; it's other states' garbage

Q: Do you support opening the national nuclear repository at Yucca Mountain?

PAUL: I've opposed this. I approach it from a state's rights position. What right does 49 states have to punish one state and say, "We're going to put our garbage in your state"? I think that's wrong. The government shouldn't be in the business of subsidizing any form of energy. Nuclear energy is a good source of energy, but they still get subsidies. Then we as politicians and the bureaucrats get involved with which state's going to get stuck with the garbage. The more the free market handles this and the more you deal with property rights and no subsidies to any form of energy, the easier this problem would be solved.

Source: GOP 2011 primary debate in Las Vegas, Oct. 18, 2011

NOTE: Yucca Mountain is a federally-owned mountain in Nevada which the federal government has proposed as a long-term repository for nuclear waste. Yucca Mountain was selected because, in theory, it is geologically stable enough to survive intact for the tens of thousands of years until the nuclear waste becomes harmless. The site was first proposed under President Reagan in 1985-1987; Congress approved it under President Bush in 2002; and then Congress canceled the program under President Obama in April 2011.

Obama on Nuclear Waste

GovWatch: Opposes Yucca Mountain
for nuclear waste storage

McCain portrays Obama as saying "no to clean, safe, nuclear energy." That's false. But there's no question that McCain is a much bigger advocate of nuclear power than Obama, who has taken a more guarded position. McCain has said that he'd work to bring 45 new nuclear power plants online by 2030, with the eventual goal of building 100 new nuclear plants. Obama has criticized that, highlighting his opposition to long-term storage of nuclear waste at the federal government's Yucca Mountain site in Nevada. "He wants to build 45 new nuclear reactors when they don't have a plan to store the waste anywhere besides right here," Obama said on June 25. McCain supports going ahead with the Yucca Mountain plan.

Obama's 2007 plan promised that he "will also lead federal efforts to look for a safe, long-term disposal solution based on objective, scientific analysis." It's inaccurate to cast Obama as an opponent, and McCain goes too far when he portrays Obama as saying "no" to nuclear.

Source: GovWatch on 2008: Washington Post analysis, June 26, 2008

Paul on Animal Rights

Scored 14% on Humane Society Scorecard on animal protection

The Humane Society 109th Congress Scorecard on animal protection scored Paul 14 out of 100, based on:

- Paul voted against the Horse Slaughter Prevention Act (HR.503): To bar slaughtering horses for human consumption.

- Paul voted for the "poison pill" Amendment delaying implementation of HR.503.

- Paul did not vote on the BLM amendment on 5/19/2005: To bar slaughtering wild horses & burros.

- Paul voted against the Pets Evacuation and Transportation Standards (PETS) Act (HR.3858): To consider the needs of people with pets and service animals in disaster planning.

- Paul did not co-sponsor the Animal Fighting Prohibition Act (S.382): To criminalize dogfighting & cockfighting.

- Paul did not co-sponsor the Downed Animal Protection Act (HR.3931): to ban "downed" (unable to walk to slaughter) cattle, pigs & sheep in human food.

- Paul did not sign the Funding Letter of 4/28/2006, to the Agriculture Appropriations Subcommittee for animal protection.

Source: Humane Society 109th Congress Scorecard, www.fund.org,
Jan 31, 2007

Obama on Animal Rights

Scored 60% on Humane Society Scorecard
on animal protection

The Humane Society 109th Congress Scorecard on animal protection issues scored Obama 60 out of 100, based on:

- Obama did not co-sponsor the Horse Slaughter Prevention Act (S.1915): To bar slaughtering horses for human consumption. Bill had 34 co-sponsors.

- Obama voted for the Horse Slaughter Amendment (9/20/2005): to stop export of horses for slaughter.

- Obama co-sponsored the Animal Fighting Prohibition Act (S.382): To criminalize dogfighting & cockfighting. The bill had 51 cosponsors & passed unanimously on 4/28/2005.

- Obama did not co-sponsor the Downed Animal Protection Act (S.1779): to ban "downed" (unable to walk to slaughter) cattle, pigs & sheep in human food. Bill had 26 cosponsors.

- Obama signed the Funding Letter to the Agriculture Appropriations Subcommittee: seeking funds for the Animal Welfare Act, Humane Methods of Slaughter Act, & federal animal fighting law. The letter was cosigned by 44 senators & sent on 5/25/2006.

Source: Humane Society 109th Congress Scorecard, www.fund.org,
Jan 31, 2007

Paul on Net Neutrality

Voted NO on establishing "network neutrality" (non-tiered Internet)

An amendment, sponsored by Rep Markey (D, MA) which establishes "network neutrality" by requiring that broadband network service providers have the following duties:

- not to block or interfere with the ability of any person to use a broadband connection to access the Internet;

- to operate its broadband network in a nondiscriminatory manner so that any person can offer or provide content and services over the broadband network with equivalent or better capability than the provider extends to itself or affiliated parties, and without the imposition of a charge for such nondiscriminatory network operation;

- if the provider prioritizes or offers enhanced quality of service to data of a particular type, to prioritize or offer enhanced quality of service to all data of that type without imposing a surcharge or other consideration for such prioritization or enhanced quality of service.

Proponents say that network neutrality ensures that everybody is treated alike with regard to use of the Internet, which has been a principle applied to Internet use since it was first originated that without network neutrality, large corporations will pay for exclusive preferential service and hence small websites will be relegated to a second tier of inferior service. Opponents say that the Markey amendment forsakes the free market in favor of government price controls, and would chill investment in broadband network, and would reduce choice for internet users.

Source: Communications, Opportunity, Promotion, & Enhancement Act;
Bill HR 5252, Amendment 987 ; vote number 239 on June 8, 2006

Obama on Net Neutrality

Ensure net neutrality: no corporate-tiered Internet

A bill to amend the communications act of 1934 to ensure net neutrality:

- Broadband service providers shall not interfere with the ability of any person to use a broadband service to access or offer any lawful content via the Internet;

- only prioritize content or services based on the type of content or services and the level of service purchased by the user, without charge for such prioritization.

Sen. DORGAN. "The issue of Internet freedom is also known as net neutrality. I have long fought in Congress against media concentration, to prevent the consolidation of control over what Americans see in the media. Now, Americans face an equally great threat to the democratic vehicle of the Internet.

"The Internet became a robust engine of economic development by enabling anyone with a good idea to connect to consumers and compete on a level playing field for consumers' business. The marketplace picked winners and losers, and not some central gatekeeper.

"But now we face a situation where the FCC has removed nondiscrimination rules that applied to Internet providers for years. This fundamentally changes the way the Internet has operated and threaten to derail the democratic nature of the Internet. American consumers and businesses will be worse off for it. This Act ensures that the Internet remains a platform that spawns innovation and economic development for generations to come.

Source: Internet Freedom Preservation Act (S.215) on Jan. 9, 2007

Paul on Outer Space Policy

Militarizing outer space impoverishes America

President Bush let it be known that we will assert our jurisdiction not only worldwide, but in space as well. The president declared that the US will determine which countries will have access to space. He has announced that outer space will be militarized and controlled by the US.

Wealth is transferred from the poor to the politically connected rich through the inflationary process. The pseudo-strength of the dollar allows endless money creation to pay the bills to police the world. In the US, the process manifests in the decline of living for the poor, the middle class, and the elderly.

The limits of our policies will be exposed by military failures, the loss of political support, and a rejection of the over-inflated US dollars used to pay our bills. The cost of runaway military spending essentially brought down the Soviet Union and soon will bring down N. Korea. We are doing the same thing.

Source: A Foreign Policy of Freedom, by Ron Paul, p.367, June 15, 2007

Obama on Outer Space Policy

Cancel moon program; develop human mission to Mars

Obama wants to end NASA's moon program, turn over space transportation to commercial companies and jump-start technologies needed for future human exploration of Mars.

NASA has been working to develop a replacement for the space shuttles, which are being retired this year after five more missions to complete construction of the orbiting International Space Station, a $100 billion project of 16 nations.

Obama's budget ends work on the shuttle follow-on vehicle, known as Orion, as well as a pair of rockets developed to fly astronauts to the space station, the moon and other destinations in the solar system.

"We are proposing canceling the program, not delaying it," said a spokesperson. Funds previously earmarked for the Constellation program, initially intended to return US astronauts to the moon by 2020, instead would be used for research projects that include robotics and other technologies needed to prepare for an eventual human mission to Mars.

Source: Reuters wire service, "Obama axes NASA moon plan",
Jan. 31, 2010

Paul on Privacy Rights

Government computer snooping
makes National ID Card inevitable

We allow the FBI and CIA to snoop on everything and everybody, and rarely is the snooping challenged on principle. The computer age is now upon us, and this technology could easily eliminate completely the privacy that should be cherished by all freedom-loving individuals. Like nuclear power, computer technology can enhance or standard of living or destroy our freedom completely. It is just a matter of time until we have a mandatory national ID card.

Source: Freedom Under Siege, by Ron Paul, p. 16-17, Dec. 31, 1987

Surveillance cameras are out of control;
safety is no excuse

The government's use of surveillance cameras is out of control. Cameras at traffic lights are pervasive throughout the country. Challenging the charges in court is frequently not even permitted. The excuse is always the same: They are providing safety for us. But unlike in the private sector, this is not really believable. Government much too often violates our privacy and at the same time is fanatical in protecting its own secrecy. Not only are the government's cameras proliferating the government itself is turning even the private camera into a threat it otherwise would not be. Under the Patriot Act, private cameras as well as cell phones are vulnerable to an aggressive federal government. Nothing good can come out of permitting government to film our every move.

Source: Liberty Defined, by Rep. Ron Paul, p.278-279, April 19, 2011

Obama on Privacy Rights

Personal privacy must be protected even in terrorism age

Americans fought a revolution in part over the right to be free from unreasonable searches, to ensure that our government couldn't come knocking in the middle of the night for no reason. We need to find a way forward to make sure that we [stop] terrorists while protecting the privacy and liberty of innocent Americans.

Source: In His Own Words, edited by Lisa Rogak, p.132, March 27, 2007

Homeland security must protect citizens, not intrude on them

Homeland security must protect citizens, not intrude on them

Every democracy is tested when it is faced with a serious threat. As a nation we have to find the right balance between privacy and security, between executive authority to face threats and uncontrolled power. What protects us are the procedures we put in place to protect that balance, namely judicial warrants and congressional review. These are concrete safeguards to make sure surveillance hasn't gone too far.

Source: In His Own Words, edited by Lisa Rogak, p. 99, March 27, 2007

Paul on Health Mandate

States *CAN* mandate insurance, but it's a bad idea

Q: [to Romney]: Where do you find mandating authority for health insurance [as RomneyCare does] in the Constitution?

ROMNEY: Are you familiar with the Massachusetts constitution? I am. It allows states [to mandate insurance].

Q: [to Paul]: Does a state has a constitutional right to make someone buy insurance just because they're a resident?

PAUL: No, the federal government can't go in and prohibit the states from doing bad things. And I would consider that a very bad thing, but you don't send in a federal police force because they're doing it. So they do have that leeway under our Constitution. But we have drifted so far from any of our care being delivered by the marketplace. And once you get the government involved—both parties have done it—they've developed a medical care delivery system based on corporatism. The corporations are doing quite well, whether it's Obama or under the Republicans. The drug companies do well. The insurance companies do well. The patient and the doctors suffer.

Source: Iowa Straw Poll 2011 GOP debate in Ames Iowa, Aug. 11, 2011

Obama on Health Mandate

Zero fines & no mandate for small business

McCAIN: Sen. Obama wants, if you've got [a small business with] employees, if you don't adopt the health care plan that Sen. Obama mandates, he's going to fine you. Now, Sen. Obama, I'd still like to know what that fine is going to be.

OBAMA: Here's your fine—zero. Zero, because as I said in our last debate and I'll repeat, I exempt small businesses from the requirement for large businesses that can afford to provide health care to their employees, but are not doing it. I exempt small businesses from having to pay into a kitty. But large businesses that can afford it, we've got a choice. Either they provide health insurance to their employees or somebody has to. Right now, what happens is those employees get dumped into either the Medicaid system, which taxpayers pick up, or they're going to the emergency room for uncompensated care, which everybody picks up in their premiums.

Source: Third presidential debate against John McCain, Oct. 15, 2008

Voluntary universal participation, like in Medicare Part B

I believe that if we make [health insurance] affordable, people will purchase it. In fact, Medicare Part B is not mandated, it is voluntary. And yet people over 65 choose to purchase it, because it's a good deal. And if people end up seeing a plan that is affordable for them, I promise you they are snatching it up because they are desperate to get health care.

Source: Democratic Debate in Cleveland, Feb. 26, 2008

Paul on Medicare

Let people opt out of Medicare

Q: How do you propose to keep Medicare financially solvent?

PAUL: Well, under these conditions, it's not solvent and won't be solvent. If you're an average couple, you would have put $140,000 into it. And in your lifetime, you will take out more than three times that much. So a little bit of arithmetic tells you it's not solvent, so we're up against the wall on that, so it can't be made solvent. It has to change. We have to have more competition in medicine.

I would think that if we don't want to cut any of the medical benefits for children or the elderly, because we have drawn so many in and got them so dependent on the government, if you want to work a transition, you have to cut a lot of money. Some revamping has to occur. What we need is competition. We need to get a chance for the people to opt out of the system. You talk about opting out of Obamacare? Why can't we opt out of the whole system and take care of ourselves?

Source: 2011 GOP primary debate in Manchester NH, June 13, 2011

Obama on Medicare

Medicare is major driver of our long-term liabilities

Pres. OBAMA: The major driver of our long-term liabilities, is Medicare and Medicaid and our health care spending. That's going to be what our children have to worry about. Now, [Rep. Paul Ryan's] approach—if I understand it correctly, would say we're going to provide vouchers of some sort for current Medicare recipients at the current level.

Rep. RYAN: No.

Pres. OBAMA: No?

Rep. RYAN: People 55 and above are grandfathered in.

Pres. OBAMA: But just for future beneficiaries, the basic idea would be that at some point we hold Medicare cost per recipient constant as a way of making sure that that doesn't go way out of whack, right?

Rep. RYAN: We drew it as a blend of inflation and health inflation. Medicare is a $38 trillion unfunded liability—it has to be reformed for younger generations because it's going bankrupt. And the premise of our idea is, why not give people the same kind of health care plan we here have in Congress?

Source: Obama Q&A at House Republican retreat, Jan. 29, 2010

Paul on ObamaCare

ObamaCare is only as socialized as Bush's & Nixon's reforms

Obama has been accused of pushing for socialized medicine. This is not exactly true. Maybe in time it will become a total government program. But actually his reforms are very similar to reforms pushed by the Republicans over the decades. The Republican Party under Eisenhower established the Department of Health, Education and Welfare in the 1950s. Nixon pushed through managed care ERISA laws in the early 1970s after a decade of Democrats implementing their Medicare and Medicaid programs with strong Republican support. The Reagan administration expanded medical transfer payments. Prescription drug programs were passed by the George Bush administration and a Republican Congress. And now it's the Democrats' turn once again. Republicans shout "socialized medicine" as they became the nominal opponents of Obama Care.

Source: Liberty Defined, by Rep. Ron Paul, p.196, April 19, 2011

Obama on ObamaCare

Repealing healthcare reform would cost $250B

The only way to tackle our deficit is to cut excessive spending wherever we find it. This means further reducing health care costs, including programs like Medicare and Medicaid, which are the single biggest contributor to our long-term deficit. The health insurance law we passed last year will slow these rising costs, which is part of the reason that nonpartisan economists have said that repealing the health care law would add a quarter of a trillion dollars to our deficit. Still, I'm willing to look at other ideas to bring down costs, including one that Republicans suggested last year—medical malpractice reform to rein in frivolous lawsuits.

Source: State of the Union speech, Jan. 26, 2011

FactCheck: ObamaCare saves $2B to $10B, not $250B

Many of the cost-saving measures the president has touted are untested, such as changes in the way care is delivered, new payment models and pilot projects that some experts applaud, and others question.

The nonpartisan Congressional Budget Office expects that for most Americans, who get their insurance through work, health insurance premium costs won't change significantly from what they would have been without the law. CBO estimated that the major parts will cost $10 billion over the 2010-2019 period, while Medicare's Office of the Actuary determined savings of only $2 billion.

Source: FactCheck.org on State of the Union speech, Jan. 26, 2011

Paul on AIDS Policy

Distribute sterile syringes to reduce AIDS and hepatitis

Paul signed the Community AIDS and Hepatitis Prevention Act: To permit the use of Federal funds for syringe exchange programs for purposes of reducing the transmission of bloodborne pathogens, including HIV and viral hepatitis.

Congress finds as follows:

- Each year, approximately 12,000 Americans contract HIV/AIDS and approximately 19,000 Americans contract the hepatitis C virus directly or indirectly from sharing contaminated syringes.

- A 2005 comprehensive international review of the evidence of the effectiveness of syringe exchange programs in preventing HIV transmission shows that such programs reduce HIV transmission and are cost-effective.

- Research has shown that injection drug users who are referred to addiction treatment from syringe exchange programs are more likely to enter and remain in treatment.

- Research has shown that, by providing safe disposal of used injection equipment, syringe exchange programs significantly reduce the number of improperly discarded syringes in the community, thereby reducing the exposure of police and others to dangers of blood-borne disease from accidental syringe sticks.

Despite the scientific and public health consensus that syringe exchange programs reduce HIV and do not increase substance abuse, a ban on funding syringe exchange has been enacted as part of each Appropriations Act since 1998.

Source: HR 179 on Jan. 6, 2009

Obama on AIDS Policy

Advocated condom use to avoid AIDS, at Saddleback Church

In Dec. 2006 Obama took part in an event at the Saddleback megachurch. It was World AIDS Day, and Obama appeared alongside Sen. Sam Brownback (R, KS). Brownback remarked, "Welcome to my house," prompting peals from the crowd. When Obama's turn came, he remarked, "There is one thing I've gotta say: This is my house, too. This is God's house." He quoted Corinthians and advocated the use of condoms to prevent the spread of HIV. The huge crowd of conservative Evangelists awarded him a standing ovation.

Source: Game Change, by Heilemann & Halpern, p. 69, Jan. 11, 2010

Got tested for AIDS, with wife, in public, in Kenya

Q: African-Americans, though 17% of all American teenagers, are 69% of the population of teenagers diagnosed with HIV/AIDS. What is the plan to protect these young people from this scourge?

BIDEN: I spent last summer going through the black sections of my town, getting people in the position where testing matters. I got tested for AIDS. I know Barack got tested for AIDS. There's no shame in being tested for AIDS.

OBAMA: I just got to make clear—I got tested with Michelle, when we were in Kenya in Africa. I don't want any confusion here about what's going on. I was tested with my wife. In public.

Source: Democratic Primary Debate at Howard University, June 28, 2007

Paul vs. Obama
on Economic Issues

Economic issues focus on the recession recovery and all fiscal matters, including the following topics:

• *Budget & Economy:* including deficit spending and all aspects of the federal budget. Rep. Paul's ideas about ending the Federal Reserve, once considered extremist, have become mainstream; he also opposes all bailouts and economic stimulus. Obama focuses instead on how to distribute the economic stimulus more fairly.

• *Corporations:* including corporate taxation and corporate welfare. Paul focuses on the dangers of concentrated power, while Obama would raise corporate taxes and taxes on high-income earners.

• *Government Reform:* focusing on the size of the federal government, which Paul thinks should be smaller and more restricted. Obama instead focuses on transparency.

• *Jobs:* including unemployment and union issues. Rep. Paul would restrict unions and limit unemployment compensation; Pres. Obama supports the opposite on both issues.

• *Social Security:* including the current Trust Fund and changes for the future. Rep. Paul would provide opt-out mechanisms; Pres. Obama opposes any form of privatization.

• *Tax Reform:* including income taxes, tax rates, and bracket redistribution. Rep. Paul would radically reduce taxes, citing libertarian limited government. Pres. Obama focuses on revenue enhancement for fairness and for fixing the economy.

Ron Paul
on Economic Issues

Barack Obama
on Economic Issues

Paul on CEO Compensation

Inflated currency benefits some industry's CEO salaries

The seekers of bailouts condemn their opponents as stubborn and selfish ideologues. Of course, when those wanting the taxpayers' bailouts were making profits, they were quite content to support the principle that the profits were theirs to keep as part of free-market philosophy.

It's not a question of being an ideologue. The ideologue label is used to make the morally principled ideology look confrontational and uncaring. This then makes it seem like the immoral philosophy, based on government force, is morally superior. It's always couched in terms of caring for the underdog & not as a bailout of those who have unfairly been benefiting from an economic system artificially stimulated by an inflated currency that benefited certain industries' CEO salaries and workers' wages and benefits.

Very simply, there can't be a more immoral system of money than one based on a banking monopoly that can counterfeit money in secret. The moral argument against the Fed should be enough to dispense with it posthaste.

Source: End the Fed, by Rep. Ron Paul, p.155-156, Sept. 29, 2010

Obama on CEO Compensation

I will raise CEO taxes, no doubt about it

Q: McCain is going to say you're going to raise taxes.

A: I will raise CEO taxes. There is no doubt about it.

Q: What about the average American?

A: If you are a CEO in this country, you will probably pay more taxes. They won't be prohibitively high. You're going to be paying roughly what you paid in the '90s, when CEOs were doing just fine.

Q: So, you want to just eliminate the Bush tax cuts?

A: I want to eliminate the Bush tax cuts. And what I have said is, I will institute a middle-class tax cut. So, if you're making $75,000, if you're making $50,000 a year, you will see an extra $1,000 a year offsetting on your payroll tax.

Q: Define middle class.

A: Well, look, I think that the definitions are always a little bit rough, but if you're making $100,000 a year or less, then you're pretty solidly middle class, and you deserve relief right now, as opposed to paying higher taxes. But people who are making over $200,000 or $250,000 have benefited the most from economic growth.

Source: CNN Late Edition: 2008 presidential series with Wolf Blitzer,
May 11, 2008

Paul on Financial Bailout

Don't bail out banks;
bail out homeowners

Q: [to Cain]: Regarding "Occupy Wall St.," you said, "Don't blame Wall Street, don't blame the big banks. If you don't have a job, and you're not rich, blame yourself." Do you still say that?

CAIN: Yes, I do still say that. They might be frustrated with Wall Street and the bankers, but they're directing their anger at the wrong place. They ought to be over in front of the White House taking out their frustration.

PAUL: I think Mr. Cain has blamed the victims. There's a lot of people that are victims of this business cycle. We can't blame the victims. I'd go to Washington as well as Wall Street, but I'd go over to the Federal Reserve. The bailouts came from both parties. The banks were involved, and the Federal Reserve was involved. But who got stuck? The middle class got stuck. They got stuck. They lost their jobs, and they lost their houses. If you had to give money out, you should have given it to people who were losing their mortgages, not to the banks.

Source: GOP 2011 primary debate in Las Vegas, Oct. 18, 2011

Obama on Financial Bailout

We all hated the bank bailout; but it was necessary

Our most urgent task upon taking office was to shore up the same banks that helped cause this crisis. It was not easy to do. And if there's one thing that has unified Democrats and Republicans, and everybody in between, it's that we all hated the bank bailout. I hated it. You hated it. It was about as popular as a root canal.

But when I ran for President, I promised I wouldn't just do what was popular—I would do what was necessary. And if we had allowed the meltdown of the financial system, unemployment might be double what it is today.

So I supported the last administration's efforts to create the financial rescue program. And when we took that program over, we made it more transparent and more accountable. And as a result, the markets are now stabilized, and we've recovered most of the money we spent on the banks. Most but not all.

To recover the rest, I've proposed a fee on the biggest banks. I am not interested in punishing banks. I'm interested in protecting our economy.

Source: State of the Union Address, Jan. 27, 2010

Paul on Wall Street Reform

Go after crony capitalism; defend real capitalism

Q: Gov. Perry's critics in the state of Texas—you're a congressman from Texas—say he practices crony capitalism as governor. Are they right?

PAUL: I haven't analyzed it enough to call him a crony or not. But there is a lot of crony capitalism going on in this country. And that has to be distinguished from real capitalism, because this "Occupation" stuff on Wall Street, if you're going after crony capitalism, I'm all for it. Those are the people who benefit from contracts from government, benefits from all of the bailouts. They don't deserve compassion, they deserve taxation, or they deserve to have all their benefits removed. But crony capitalism isn't when somebody makes money and they produce a product. That is very important. We have to distinguish the two. And unfortunately, I think some people mix that. But this, to me, is so vital, that we recognize what capitalism is versus crony capitalism. When you have crony capitalism, and that's why we're facing this crisis today.

Source: CNBC GOP Primary debate in Rochester MI, Nov. 9, 2011

Obama on Wall Street Reform

Pay attention to Main Street, not just Wall Street

OBAMA: Unless we are holding ourselves accountable day-in, day-out, not just when there's a crisis for folks who have power and influence and can hire lobbyists but for the nurse, the teacher, the police officer who frankly at the end of each month, they've got a little financial crisis going on. They're having to take out extra debt just to make their mortgage payments. We haven't been paying attention to them.

McCAIN: We've got fundamental problems in the system. And Main Street is paying a penalty for the excesses and greed in Washington and on Wall Street. We have a long way to go.

Q: Are you going to vote for the Senate bailout plan?

McCAIN: Sure. But there's also the issue of responsibility. I've been criticized for calling for the resignation of the SEC chairman. We've got to start also holding people accountable.

OBAMA: McCain's absolutely right that we need more responsibility, but we need it not just when there is a crisis. We've had years in which the reigning economic ideology has been what's good for Wall Street but not what's good for Main Street. There are folks out there who have been struggling before this crisis took place. And that's why it's so important we look at some of the underlying issues that have led to wages and incomes for ordinary Americans to go down, a health care system that is broken, energy policies that are not working. Unless we are holding ourselves accountable day-in, day-out, not just when there's a crisis for folks who have power and influence and can hire lobbyists.

Source: First presidential debate, Obama vs. McCain, Sept. 26, 2008

Paul on Economic Stimulus

Stimulus package means more printing
& devaluing the dollar

What is the bailout package all about? Our side of the aisle proposes it and the Democrats want to increase it. $150 billion? No, let's up it $200 billion! Where does it come from?—the government has no money. Well, can we tax people?—no, you can't tax anymore. What are they gonna do?—they're gonna print the money, devalue the dollar, & that's the problem we have.

The dollar is low, prices are high, the people are suffering, the middle class is shrinking. So we offer the same old pabulum, the same old baloney, and then we turn around and say, "Well, why don't we ask the Federal Reserve to create more money? Nobody seems to have enough money. If we just had more money, maybe it would prop up the stock market." So we go to the Federal Reserve and say we need more money. So they crank it out. You can't lower interest rates unless you print more money. So they lower interest rates dramatically, like never before. So we're in a bind, we're in a fix, and I'll tell you what: we overspend. Everywhere!

Source: Speeches to 2008 Conservative Political Action Conference,
Feb 7, 2008

Obama on Economic Stimulus

$1T avoided Depression; but I took office with $8T debt

Let me start the discussion of government spending by setting the record straight. At the beginning of the last decade, the year 2000, America had a budget surplus of over $200 billion. By the time I took office, we had a one-year deficit of over $1 trillion and projected deficits of $8 trillion over the next decade. Most of this was the result of not paying for two wars, two tax cuts, and an expensive prescription drug program. On top of that, the effects of the recession put a $3 trillion hole in our budget. All this was before I walked in the door.

Just stating the facts. Now, if we had taken office in ordinary times, I would have liked nothing more than to start bringing down the deficit. But we took office amid a crisis. And our efforts to prevent a second depression have added another $1 trillion to our national debt. That, too, is a fact. I'm absolutely convinced that was the right thing to do.

Source: State of the Union Address, Jan. 27, 2010

Paul on Trickle-Down Economics

1980s had huge deficits, despite Reagan's message

PERRY: You wrote a letter to Ronald Reagan and said I'm going to quit the party because of the things you believe in.

PAUL: I strongly supported Ronald Reagan. I was one of four members of Congress from Texas that supported Reagan in '76. And I supported him all along, and I supported all his issues and all his programs. But in the 1980s, we spent too much, we taxed too much, we built up our deficits, and it was a bad scene. Therefore, I support the message of Ronald Reagan. The message was great. But the consequence, we have to be honest with ourselves. It was not all that great. Huge deficits during the 1980s, and that is what my criticism was for, not for Ronald Reagan's message. His message is a great message.

Source: 2011 GOP debate in Simi Valley CA at the Reagan Library,
Sep 7, 2011

Obama on Trickle-Down Economics

Not enough to help those at the top: it doesn't trickle down

Q: How can we bail people out of economic ruin?

OBAMA: It's not enough just to help those at the top. Prosperity is not just going to trickle down. We've got to help the middle class. Part of the problem is that for many of you, wages and incomes have flat-lined. For many of you, it is getting harder and harder to save, harder and harder to retire. Sen. McCain is right that we've got to stabilize housing prices. But underlying that is loss of jobs and loss of income. That's something that the next treasury secretary is going to have to work on.

McCAIN: We obviously have to stop this spending spree that's going on in Washington. Do you know that we've laid a $10 trillion debt on young Americans?

Source: Second presidential debate against John McCain, Oct. 7, 2008

Bottom-up economics instead of trickle-down economics

Obama explained that a healthy economy is a bottom-up economy, not a top-down economy dependent on trickle-down economics. In a bottom-up economy, the rules of business and government are fair and apply to all. There is a level playing field. Obama believes that all will benefit from the system he envisions, that Wall Street & Main Street are intertwined, that you can't have successful companies without motivated engaged workers

Source: Obamanomics, by John R. Talbott, p. 18-19, July 1, 2008

Paul on National Debt

We've come to accept debt, wealth confiscation, and big government

We have been conditioned to accept debt as part of every aspect of our lives. The short-term benefit of government borrowing is a political expediency that, in spite of the rhetoric of the balanced budget, is growing ever more popular.

Sadly, we rarely hear serious proposals for limiting the role of government to that of protecting liberty.

In the 20th century we have come to accept demands and needs as rights at the expense of someone else's rights. Responsibility for our own acts and livelihood has been replaced by lawsuits demanding unrealistic settlements.

Government has come to mean something entirely different than what was intended by the writers of the Constitution. It is an entity capable of confiscating and distributing wealth ad infinitum. Government no longer serves the people by guaranteeing equal rights to all. Government is now expected to provide profits, medical care, jobs, homes, and food whenever the people demand these benefits as a right.

Source: Freedom Under Siege, by Ron Paul, p. 2, Dec. 31, 1987

Obama on National Debt

Freeze annual domestic spending for next five years

Now that the worst of the recession is over, we have to confront the fact that our government spends more than it takes in. That is not sustainable. Every day, families sacrifice to live within their means. They deserve a government that does the same.

This freeze will require painful cuts. Already, we've frozen the salaries of hardworking federal employees for the next two years. I've proposed cuts to things I care deeply about, like community action programs. The Secretary of Defense has also agreed to cut tens of billions of dollars in spending that he and his generals believe our military can do without.

Source: State of the Union speech, Jan. 26, 2011

Paul on Balanced Budget

Supports Balanced Budget Amendment
& on-budget accounting

Paul adopted the Republican Liberty Caucus Position Statement:

The Republican Liberty Caucus endorses the following [among its] principles:

- There should be an amendment to the US Constitution to require a balanced budget, provided it includes a supermajority requirement to raise taxes and provided it does not empower the judiciary to unilaterally raise taxes.

- Honest accounting dictates that all federal expenditures should be on budget.

- Each budget should be derived based upon the justification for and needs of each program, with no program being either budgeted for or increased automatically.

Source: Republican Liberty Caucus Position Statement, Dec. 8, 2000

Obama on Balanced Budget

Appoint bipartisan fiscal commission and re-establish PAYGO

We know that we've got a major fiscal challenge in reining in deficits that have been growing for a decade, and threaten our future. That's why I've proposed a three-year freeze in discretionary spending other than what we need for national security.

At this point, we know that the budget surpluses of the '90s occurred in part because of the pay-as-you-go law, which said that, well, you should pay as you go and live within our means, just like families do every day. 24 Republicans voted for that, and I appreciate it. And we were able to pass it in the Senate yesterday.

But the idea of a bipartisan fiscal commission to confront the deficits in the long term died in the Senate the other day. So I'm going to establish such a commission by executive order and I hope that you participate, fully and genuinely, in that effort, because if we're going to actually deal with our deficit and debt.

Source: Obama Q&A at 2010 House Republican retreat in Baltimore ,
Jan. 29, 2010

NOTE: "PAYGO" refers to a "pay-as-you-go" policy, where all expenditures in a bill are explicitly paid for, instead of requiring borrowing. The Budget Enforcement Act of 1990 required all new spending bills to include how the spending would be balanced by revenue enhancements (taxes or fees) or other spending cuts. The PAYGO statute expired in 2002, but some congressional bills still describe offsets for new spending.

Paul on Earmarks

Put 65 projects into 2006 bills, worth $4B to his district

Q: You talk about opposing big government, but you seem to have a different attitude about your own congressional district. In 2006, your district received more than $4 billion: 65 earmark-targeted projects that you have put into congressional bills for your district.

A: You got it completely wrong. I've never voted for an earmark in my life.

Q: No, but you put them in the bill.

A: I put it in because I represent people who are asking for some of their money back.

Q: If you put it in the bill, and then you know it's going to pass Congress and so you don't refuse the money.

A: Well, no, of course not. It's like taking a tax credit. I'm against the taxes but I take all my tax credits. I want to get the money back for the people.

Q: If you were true to your philosophy, you would say no pork spending in my district.

A: No, no, that's not it. They steal our money, that's like saying that people shouldn't take Social Security money. I'm trying to save the system, make the system work

Source: Meet the Press: 2007 "Meet the Candidates" series,
Dec 23, 2007

Obama on Earmarks

Some earmarks are defensible, if done in full light of day

Rep. CHAFFETZ: When you said in the House of Representatives that you were going to tackle earmarks—in fact, you didn't want to have any earmarks in any of your bills—I jumped up out of my seat and applauded you. But it didn't happen.

Pres. OBAMA: We didn't have earmarks in the Recovery Act. We didn't get a lot of credit for it, but there were no earmarks in that. I was confronted at the beginning of my term with an omnibus package that did have a lot of earmarks from Republicans and Democrats when we had to make a whole bunch of emergency decisions about the economy. So what I said was let's keep them to a minimum, but I couldn't excise them all. I think all of us are willing to acknowledge that some earmarks are perfectly defensible, good projects; it's just they haven't gone through the regular appropriations process in the full light of day. So one place to start is to make sure that they are at least transparent, that everybody knows what's there before we move forward.

Source: Obama Q&A at House Republican retreat in Baltimore,
Jan 29, 2010

NOTE: "Earmarks" refers to itemized spending in legislation, i.e., funding targeted toward a particular project in a particular place. The controversy comes about because often the particular place includes the home district of the legislator writing or sponsoring the bill (which is known derisively as "Pork-Barrel Spending"). Earmarks are currently legal and are generally considered ethical; earmark reform focuses on publicizing their existence and perhaps on a future Line Item Veto to remove some.

Paul on Unions

Right to organize; but no special benefits for unions

Q: Are unions good for America?

A: The right to unionize should be a basic right of any group. You should be able to organize. You should have no privileges, no special benefits legislated to benefit the unions, but you should never deny any working group to organize and negotiate for the best set of standards of working conditions.

Source: 2007 Republican debate in Dearborn, Michigan, Oct. 9, 2007

Mandated wages & unions hurt unprotected workers

Minimum wage laws & mandating union contracts (closed shop) are designed to help a small segment of workers gain economic advantage while actually hurting unprotected workers. Long term, even the beneficiaries suffer from the unemployment that excessive wage demands bring about.

Coerced union wages and dictated minimum wages grossly distort the market process and contribute to the malinvestment initiated by the Federal Reserve policy and guarantee that in the correction, wages must come down.

Source: Liberty Defined, by Rep. Ron Paul, p.309-310, April 19, 2011

Obama on Unions

FactCheck: Yes, wants to limit secret balloting for unions

The Statement:

In a speech at Virginia Beach, McCain took on Obama's stance on unions: "Obama is planning to take away your right to vote by secret ballot in labor elections," he said.

The Facts:

McCain is referring to a plan supported by labor unions. Currently, workers must get at least 30% of their colleagues to sign an authorization form to ask for union representation—then hold a secret-ballot vote to finalize it. The change Obama supports, part of the Employee Free-Choice Act, would let a union be recognized by the National Labor Relations Board immediately after the majority signs the authorization. Supporters of the change say it would cut down on the ability of employers to pressure their workers to vote against a union.

The Verdict:

True. McCain accurately represents Obama's stance, although they disagree on the merits of the plan. Organized labor backs Obama's position, while business groups & some non-union workers support McCain's.

Source: CNN FactCheck on 2008 presidential race, Oct. 13, 2008

Paul on Unemployment Extension

Voted NO on extending unemployment benefits from 39 weeks to 59 weeks

Congressional Summary: Revises the formula for Tier-1 amounts a state credits to an applicant's emergency unemployment compensation account. Increases the figures in the formula from 50% to 80% of the total amount of regular compensation; and from 13 to 20 times the individual's average weekly benefit amount.

Proponent's argument to vote Yes:

Rep. CHARLES RANGEL (D, NY-15): Over the last 12 months the number of unemployed workers has jumped by over 2 million, leaving 10 million Americans struggling for work. These are hardworking people that have lost their jobs through no fault of their own.

Rep. JERRY WELLER (R, IL-11): This program continues the requirement that those benefiting from extended unemployment benefits had to have worked at least 20 weeks. Americans were rightly concerned about proposals to eliminate that work requirement and allow 39 weeks or, under the legislation before us today, as many as 59 weeks of total unemployment benefits to be paid to those who have previously only worked for a few weeks.

Opponent's argument to vote No:

None voiced.

Source: Unemployment Compensation Extension Act; Bill HR.6867;
vote number 683, Oct. 3, 2008

Obama on Unemployment Extension

$4,000 tax credit for companies
who hire unemployed workers

The purpose of the American Jobs Act is simple: to put more people back to work and more money in the pockets of those who are working. It will create more jobs for construction workers, more jobs for teachers, more jobs for veterans, and more jobs for the long-term unemployed. It will provide a tax break for companies who hire new workers, and it will cut payroll taxes in half for every working American and every small business. It will provide a jolt to an economy that has stalled, and give companies confidence that if they invest and hire, there will be customers for their products and services. You should pass this jobs plan right away.

Pass this jobs bill, and starting tomorrow, small businesses will get a tax cut if they hire new workers or raise workers' wages. Pass this jobs bill, and companies will get a $4,000 tax credit if they hire anyone who has spent more than six months looking for a job. We have to do more to help the long-term unemployed in their search for work.

Source: Pres. Obama's 2011 Jobs Speech, Sept. 8, 2011

Paul on Social Security Privatization

System is broke; allow young people to get out

Q: Is Social Security a Ponzi scheme?

PAUL: Well, I agree that Social Security is broke. We spent all the money and it's on its last legs unless we do something. One bill that I had in Congress—never got passed—was to prevent the Congress from spending any of that money on the wars and all the nonsense that we do around the world. Now the other thing that I would like to see done is a transition. I think it's terrible that the Social Security system has the problems it has, but if people wouldn't have spent the money we would be OK. Now, what I would like to do is to allow all the young people to get out of Social Security and go on their own. Now, the big question is, is how would the funding occur?

Source: 2011 GOP Tea Party debate in Tampa FL, Sept. 12, 2011

Obama on Social Security Privatization

What do we do with the losers of privatizing?

"What would the Ownership Society do with the losers (if Social Security were privatized)? Unless we're willing to see seniors starve on the streets, we're going to have to cover their retirement expenses one way or another—and since we don't know in advance which of us will be losers, it makes sense for all of us to chip into a pool that gives us at least some guaranteed income in our golden years. That doesn't mean we shouldn't encourage individuals to pursue higher-risk, higher-return investment strategies. They should. It just means that they should do so with savings other than those put into Social Security."

Thus, Obama sees the key underlying fallacy of privatization proposals. If we allow people to invest in riskier assets in the stock market, we will just have more losers who end up gambling with their retirement money and end up with nothing at retirement.

Source: Obamanomics, by John R. Talbott, p.161, July 1, 2008

Privatization puts retirement at whim of stock market

Q: Would you raise the cap for Social Security tax above the current level of the first $97,500 worth of income?

A: I think that lifting the [$97,500 income] cap is probably going to be the best option. My personal view is that lifting the cap is much preferable to the other options that are available. And we should reject things that will weaken the system, including privatization, which essentially is going to put people's retirement at the whim of the stock market.

Source: Democratic primary debate at Dartmouth College, Sept. 6, 2007

Paul on Trust Fund

Never voted to spend one penny
of Social Security money

Q: You said in 1988 that you would abolish Social Security. You're OK with Social Security now?

A: I think we need to offer the kids the chance to get out. But right now, if we don't save the money, we can't take care of the other. I never voted to spend one penny of Social Security money. So I'm the one that has saved it. I say take that money—and I say this constantly—don't turn anybody out on the streets—people we have conditioned—but I would say take care of the people that are dependent on us. The only way you can do that is cut spending. If we don't, they're all going to be out in the street. Because right now Social Security beneficiaries are getting 2% raises, but their cost of living is going up 10%. A dollar crisis is going to wipe them all out.

Source: Meet the Press: 2007 "Meet the Candidates" series,
Dec 23, 2007

Obama on Trust Fund

Must capture new revenue;
no new Social Security Commission

OBAMA: We're going to have to capture some revenue in order to stabilize the Social Security system. You can't get something for nothing. And if we care about Social Security, which I do, and if we are firm in our commitment to make sure that it's going to be there for the next generation, and not just for our generation, then we have an obligation to figure out how to stabilize the system. I think we should be honest in presenting our ideas in terms of how we're going to do that and not just say that we're going to form a commission and try to solve the problem some other way.

CLINTON: With all due respect, the last time we had a crisis in Social Security was 1983. President Reagan and Speaker Tip O'Neill came up with a commission. That was the best and smartest way, because you've got to get Republicans and Democrats together. That's what I will do.

OBAMA: That commission raised the retirement age, and also raised the payroll tax. So Sen. Clinton can't have it both ways.

Source: Philadelphia primary debate, on eve of PA primary, April 16, 2008

Paul on Tax-and-Spend Policies

Tax code is the symptom; spending is the problem

Q: In your tax plan, you want to close down agencies. Where do those jobs go?

A: Eventually they go into the private sector. Then don't all leave immediately when the plan goes into effect. But what my plan does is it addresses taxes in a little different way. We are talking about the tax code. But that's the consequence, that's the symptom.

The disease is spending. Every time you spend, spending is a tax. We tax the people, we borrow, and then we print the money and the prices go up, and that is a tax. So you have to address the subject of spending. That is the tax.

That is the reason I go after the spending. I propose in the first year cut $1 trillion out of the budget in 5 departments. Now the other thing is that you must do if you want to get the economy going and going again is you have to get rid of price-fixing. And the most significant price-fixing that goes on, that gave us the bubble and destroyed the economy, is the price-fixing of the Federal Reserve.

Source: 2011 CNBC GOP Primary debate in Rochester Michigan,
Nov. 9, 2011

Obama on Tax-and-Spend Policies

We need a tax code where everybody pays their fair share

I'm well aware that there are many Republicans who don't believe we should raise taxes on those who are most fortunate and can best afford it. But here is what every American knows. While most people in this country struggle to make ends meet, a few of the most affluent citizens and corporations enjoy tax breaks and loopholes that nobody else gets. Right now, Warren Buffet pays a lower tax rate than his secretary—an outrage he has asked us to fix. We need a tax code where everyone gets a fair shake, and everybody pays their fair share.

Source: Pres. Obama's 2011 Jobs Speech, Sept. 8, 2011

2011 budget calls for top bracket of 39.6% to replace 35%

Right now, the top marginal tax rate is about 42% (35% federal, 2.9% Medicare, and an average of 4% of state and local income taxes). But Obama's tax plans will send our top marginal rate skyrocketing.

Obviously, Obama and Congress are going to push for increases on taxes for the wealthy. In his 2011 budget, Obama calls for going back to the pre-Bush top bracket of 39.6% from the current level of 35%.

Source: Take Back America, by Dick Morris, p. 63-64, April 13, 2010

Paul on Death Tax

Phaseout the death tax

Paul co-sponsored the Death Tax Elimination Act:

Title: To amend the Internal Revenue Code of 1986 to phaseout the estate and gift taxes over a 10-year period.

Summary: Repeals, effective January 1, 2011, current provisions relating to the basis of property acquired from a decedent. Provides with respect to property acquired from a decedent dying on January 1, 2011, or later that:

- property shall be treated as transferred by gift; and

- the basis of the person acquiring the property shall be the lesser of the adjusted basis of the decedent or the fair market value of the property at the date of the decedent's death.

Requires specified information to be reported concerning non-cash assets over $1.3 million transferred at death and certain gifts exceeding $25,000.

Makes the exclusion of gain on the sale of a principal residence available to heirs.

Revises current provisions concerning the transfer of farm real to provide that gain on such exchange shall be recognized to the estate only to the extent that the fair market value of such property exceeds such value on the date of death.

Source: House Resolution Sponsorship HR8 on March 14, 2001

Obama on Death Tax

2011 budget proposed to raise Death Tax to 45%

One likely candidate for an increase is the so-called Death Tax—the inheritance tax that has fallen to zero in 2010 due to the schedule of Bush tax cuts passed in 2001. In his 2011 budget, Obama proposes to hike the tax back up to 45% in 2011 and apply it to all estates worth more than $3.5 million. So, if you're planning to die soon, you'd better go to your Maker in 2010—while the tax is still at zero!

The problem with the Death Tax isn't how it affects families that own the wealth so much as how it impacts those who earn money to accumulate it. The tax itself is paid by only the top 2% of families. The central question for wealthy elderly Americans is what to do with their money. Should they keep it in cash or easily liquefied investments, or is it better to plow the money back into their businesses?

The Death Tax creates an incentive *not* to invest money in one's business, but to keep it in things like houses and yachts and luxury goods—or cash and gold and bonds—that are easier to liquidate.

Source: Take Back America, by Dick Morris, p. 65-66, April 13, 2010

Paul vs. Obama on Social Issues

Social issues focus on matters which are based primarily on moral values, including the following topics:

- *Abortion:* including stem cells, partial birth, and state-level restrictions. This topic has always been the most viewed topic on our website www.OnTheIssues.org, so we explore several aspects. Paul, a medical doctor, opposes abortion on medical grounds; Obama supports abortion rights but it's not his major focus.

- *Civil Rights:* including gay rights and minority rights. For the 2012 race, gay rights will dominate this category. Rep. Paul wants government out of marriage, including gay marriage, and out of running businesses, including racial hiring decisions. Obama moved gay rights forward and would like to move beyond race-based affirmative action.

- *Education:* including college funding issues, school vouchers, and school prayer. Rep. Paul wants the federal government out of college loans, out of school funding, and out of school prayer. Obama opposes vouchers, but supports charters and more federal spending on education.

- *Families and Children:* including father's rights and family values; not a key focus for either candidate.

- *Principles and Values:* including religious issues and racism issues. This category includes the "revolution" aspects of both candidates: Obama as the first black president and Paul as a founder of the Tea Party.

- *Welfare and Poverty:* including homelessness, welfare payments, and other poverty programs. Paul wants the federal government out of providing welfare; Obama wants to keep it in.

Ron Paul on Social Issues

Barack Obama on Social Issues

Paul on Abortion Morality

Abortion causes inconsistent moral basis for value of life

In the 1960s when abortion was still illegal, I witnessed, as an OB/GYN resident, the abortion of a fetus that weighed approximately 2 pounds. It was placed in a bucket, crying and struggling to breathe, and the medical personnel pretended not to notice. Soon the crying stopped. This harrowing event forced me to think more seriously about this important issue.

That same day in the OB suite, an early delivery occurred and the infant boy was only slightly larger than the one that was just aborted. But in this room everybody did everything conceivable to save this child's life.

My conclusion that day was that we were overstepping the bounds of morality by picking and choosing who should live and who should die. There was no consistent moral basis to the value of life under these circumstances. Some people believe that being pro-choice is being on the side of freedom. I've never understood how killing a human being, albeit a small one in a special place, is portrayed as a precious right.

Source: Liberty Defined, by Rep. Ron Paul, p. 1, April 19, 2011

Obama on Abortion Morality

Moral accusations from pro-lifers are counterproductive

Q: [to Keyes]: Doesn't your pro-life stance conflict with your support of the death penalty?

ALAN KEYES: It doesn't conflict at all. Abortion and capital punishment are at different level of moral concern. Abortion is intrinsically, objectively wrong and sinful whereas capital punishment is a matter of judgment, which is not in and of itself a violation of moral right. The question of whether or not you should apply capital punishment depends on circumstances and it's an area where Catholics have a right to debate and disagree.

OBAMA: Now I agree with Mr. Keyes that the death penalty and abortion are separate cases. It's unfortunate that with the death penalty Mr. Keyes respects that people may have a different point of view but with the issue of abortion he has labeled people everything as terrorists to slaveholders to being consistent with Nazism for holding an opposing point of view. That kind of rhetoric is not helpful in resolving a deeply emotional subject.

Source: Illinois Senate Debate #3: Barack Obama vs. Alan Keyes,
Oct 21, 2004

Paul on Stem Cells

Embryonic stem cell programs not constitutionally authorized

Q: Would you expand federal funding of embryonic stem cell research?

A: Programs like this are not authorized under the Constitution. The trouble with issues like this is, in Washington we either prohibit it or subsidize it. And the market should deal with it, and the states should deal with it.

Source: GOP primary debate, at Reagan library, May 3, 2007

Voted NO on allowing human embryonic stem cell research

To provide for human embryonic stem cell research. A YES vote would:

- Call for stem cells to be taken from human embryos that were donated from in vitro fertilization clinics

- Require that before the embryos are donated, that it be established that they were created for fertility treatment and in excess of clinical need and otherwise would be discarded

- Stipulate that those donating the embryos give written consent and do not receive any compensation for the donation.

Source: Stem Cell Research Enhancement Act; Bill HR 810 ;
vote number 204 on May 24, 2005

Obama on Stem Cells

Stem cells hold promise to cure 70 major diseases

Barack Obama believes we owe it to the American public to explore the potential of stem cells to treat the millions of people suffering from debilitating and life threatening diseases. Stem cells hold the promise of treatments and cures for more than 70 major diseases and conditions such as Parkinson's and Alzheimer's disease, spinal cord injuries, and diabetes. As many as 100 million Americans may benefit from embryonic stem cell research. As president, Obama would:

- Promote Embryonic Stem Cell Research

- Support Medical Advancement and Innovation

- Expand the Number of Stem Cell Lines Available for Research

- Ensure Ethical Standards

Obama introduced legislation in the Illinois Senate to ensure that only those embryos that would otherwise be discarded could be used and that donors would have to provide written consent for the use of the embryos.

Source: Campaign website, BarackObama.com, "Resource Flyers,"
Aug 26, 2007

Notes: Stem Cells are undifferentiated cells, which are useful in disease research. Stem cells are best taken from human fetuses; hence the pro-life opposition. Many pro-life advocates support fetal stem cell research because of the medical potential. In 2001, Pres. Bush announced that the federal policy would be to allow fetal stem cell research on existing stem cell lines but not on new ones.

Paul on Judicial Activism

Nominate only judges who refuse
to legislate from the bench

Q: Will you nominate only judges who are demonstrably faithful to the judicial role of following only the text of the Constitution, and who not only refuse to legislate from the bench, but are committed to reversing prior court decision where activist judges strayed from the judicial role and legislated from the bench?

HUCKABEE: Yes.

TANCREDO: Yes.

COX: Yes.

BROWNBACK: Yes.

PAUL: Yes.

HUNTER: Yes.

KEYES: Yes.

Source: 2007 GOP Values Voter Presidential Debate, Sept. 17, 2007

Obama on Judicial Activism

No litmus test; nominate to Court based on their fairness

Q: Could you ever nominate someone to the Supreme Court who disagrees with you on Roe v. Wade?

McCAIN: I would never, and have never in all the years I've been there, imposed a litmus test on any nominee to the Court. That's not appropriate to do.

OBAMA: Well, I think it's true that we shouldn't apply a strict litmus test and the most important thing in any judge is their capacity to provide fairness and justice to the American people. And it is true that this is going to be, I think, one of the most consequential decisions of the next president. It is very likely that one of us will be making at least one and probably more than one appointments and Roe vs. Wade probably hangs in the balance. I will look for those judges who have an outstanding judicial record, who have the intellect, and who hopefully have a sense of what real-world folks are going through.

Source: Third presidential debate against John McCain, Oct. 15, 2008

Paul on Welfare State

Welfare state isn't in the Constitution

Q: A long time ago, a fellow Texan was horrified to see young kids coming into the classroom hungry. The young student teacher later went on to be President Lyndon Johnson. Providing nutrition at schools for children—is that a role of the federal government

PAUL: Well, I'm sure, when he did that, he did it with local government, and there's no rules against that. That'd be fine. But that doesn't imply that you want to endorse the entire welfare state. No; it isn't authorized in the Constitution for us to run a welfare state. And it doesn't work. All it's filled up with is mandates. But, yes, if there are poor people in Texas, we have a responsibility—I'd like to see it as voluntary as possible—but under our Constitution, our states have that right—if they feel the obligation, they have a perfect right to. This whole idea that there's something wrong with people who don't lavish out free stuff from the federal government somehow aren't compassionate enough. I resist those accusations.

Source: 2011 GOP debate in Simi Valley CA at the Reagan Library,
Sep 7, 2011

Obama on Welfare State

Cut poverty in half in 10 years, with faith-based help

Q: In the faith community, we want a new commitment around a measurable goal, something like cutting poverty in half in 10 years. Would you commit to such a goal?

A: I absolutely will make that commitment. I make that commitment with humility because we've got a lot of work to do economically in this country to bring about a more just and fair economy. We've got to shore up the mortgage market. We're going to have to change our tax code. It is a moral imperative to provide health care to every single American. And invest in early childhood education. Many of these can be part of faith-based initiatives I want to keep the Office of Faith-Based Initiatives open, but I want to make sure that its mission is clear. Faith-based initiatives should be targeted specifically at the issue of poverty and how to lift people up.

Source: Democratic Compassion Forum at Messiah College, April 13, 2008

Welfare policies contributed to erosion of black families

A lack of economic opportunity among black men, and the shame and frustration that came from not being able to provide for one's family, contributed to the erosion of black families—a problem that welfare policies for many years may have worsened. And the lack of basic services in so many urban black neighborhoods—parks for kids to play in, police walking the beat, regular garbage pickup, building code enforcement—all helped create a cycle of violence, blight and neglect that continues to haunt us.

Source: Speech on Race, in Change We Can Believe In, p.223-4,
Mar 18, 2008

Paul on Don't-Ask-Don't-Tell

Don't ask, don't tell is a decent policy for gays in army

Q: Most of our closest allies, including Great Britain and Israel, allow gays and lesbians to openly serve in the military. Is it time to end "Don't ask, don't tell" policy and allow gays and lesbians to serve openly in the US military?

A: I think the current policy is a decent policy. And the problem that we have with dealing with this subject is we see people as groups, as they belong to certain groups and that they derive their rights as belonging to groups. We don't get our rights because we're gays or women or minorities. We get our rights from our creator as individuals. So every individual should be treated the same way. So if there is homosexual behavior in the military that is disruptive, it should be dealt with. But if there's heterosexual sexual behavior that is disruptive, it should be dealt with. So it isn't the issue of homosexuality, it's the concept and the understanding of individual rights. If we understood that, we would not be dealing with this very important problem.

Source: 2007 GOP debate at Saint Anselm College, June 3, 2007

Obama on Don't-Ask-Don't-Tell

Repeal Don't-Ask-Don't-Tell

Obama believes we need to repeal the "don't ask, don't tell" policy in consultation with military commanders. The key test for military service should be patriotism, a sense of duty, and a willingness to serve. Obama will work with military leaders to repeal the current policy and ensure we accomplish our national defense goals.

Source: Campaign website, BarackObama.com, "Resource Flyers,"
Aug 26, 2007

NOTE: The policy banning open homosexuals serving in the military was repealed on Sept. 20, 2011. Hence gay and lesbian people may now openly serve in the US military. Since 1993, the DADT policy held that homosexuals may serve as long as they do not announce their homosexuality ("Don't Tell"), but also that the military may not investigate their homosexuality ("Don't Ask").

Paul on Defense of Marriage Act

No need for Marriage Amendment; DOMA is enough

Q: Will you support a federal marriage amendment, and what else will you do to protect the institution of marriage?

A: I think the best thing the president can do is set a good example, and I would start with having been married 50 years, and proud of it. I believe, also, that I do not see any need for another constitutional amendment. I think we have fallen into a trap that we have to redefine marriage. We're on the defensive, defining marriage. Why don't you just tell them to look it up in the dictionary, to find out what a marriage says? For federal legal purposes, the Defense of Marriage Act is proper. It takes care of all the problems. If you have to have rules and regulations, put it at the state level, like the Constitution says. But you know, marriage only came about and getting licenses only came about in recent history for health reasons. Marriage is a church function. It's not a state function. I don't think you need a license to get married.

Source: 2007 GOP Values Voter Presidential Debate, Sept. 17, 2007

NOTE: "DOMA" refers to the Defense of Marriage Act, passed by Congress in 1996, which defined marriage as consisting of one man and one woman (in other words, barring same-sex marriage). DOMA applies to all federal benefits and taxes, but not necessarily to state benefits and taxes.

Obama on Defense of Marriage Act

Decisions about marriage should be left to the states

One of Obama's pragmatic stands troubling to progressives is on gay marriage. In the Senate debate, Obama opposed the right-wing Federal Marriage Amendment to ban gay marriage nationally and said: "I agree with most Americans, with Democrats and Republicans, with Vice President Cheney, with over 2,000 religious leaders of all different beliefs, that decisions about marriage, as they always have, should be left to the states." However, Obama also declared, "Personally, I do believe that marriage is between a man and a woman." At the same time, Obama has strongly supported civil unions, arguing that it is a way to protect equal rights without taking the politically risky approach of gay marriage.

Source: The Improbable Quest, by John K. Wilson, p.114-115,
Oct 30, 2007

Marriage not a human right; non-discrimination is

Q: Do you think marriage is a human right?

A: I don't think marriage is a civil right, but I think that not being discriminated against is a civil right. I think making sure that we don't engage in the sort of gay-bashing that, I think, has unfortunately dominated this campaign-not just here in Illinois, but across the country-is unfortunate, and that kind of mean-spirited attacks on homosexuals is something that the people of Illinois generally have rejected.

Source: IL Senate Debate, Oct. 26, 2004

Paul on Affirmative Action

No affirmative action for any group

All rights are individuals. We do not get our rights because we belong to a group. Whether it's homosexuals, women, minorities, it leads us astray. You don't get your rights belonging to your group. A group can't force themselves on anybody else. So there should be no affirmative action for any group.

This violates the principle on the importance of the individual, and confuses us about the importance of individual rights, which is the purpose of the Constitution. Defend our individual rights.

Source: 2007 GOP Values Voter Presidential Debate, Sept. 17, 2007

Obama on Affirmative Action

Include class-based affirmative action with race-based

Obama declared his daughters "should probably be treated by any admissions officer as folks who are pretty advantaged. I think that we should take into account white kids who have been disadvantaged and have grown up in poverty and shown themselves to have what it takes to succeed."

But Obama is not race blind, and neither is his ideal of affirmative action, which would combine both race-based and class-based preferences. He said, "I don't think those concepts are mutually exclusive. I think what one can say is that in our society race and class still intersect, and there are a lot of African American kids who are struggling, that even those who are in the middle class may be first generation as opposed to fifth or sixth generation college attendees, and that we all have an interest in bringing as many people together to help build this country."

Source: The Improbable Quest, by John K. Wilson, p. 65-66, Oct. 30, 2007

Racial equality good for America as a whole

Q: Is race still the most intractable issue in America?

A: We have made enormous progress, but the progress we have made is not good enough. We live in a society that remains separated in terms of life opportunities for African-Americans, for Latinos, and the rest of the nation. But there has also got to be a social responsibility, there has to be a sense of mutual responsibility, and there's got to be political will in the White House to make that happen.

Source: Democratic Primary Debate at Howard University, June 28, 2007

Paul on College Loans

Student loan program is
a total failure and unconstitutional

Q: We are looking at student loan debt that is near $1 trillion. How would you make college more affordable?

PAUL: Well, I think you proved that the policy of student loans is a total failure. I mean, a trillion dollars of debt? And what have they gotten? A poorer education and costs that have skyrocketed because of inflation, and they don't have jobs. There's nothing more dramatically failing than that program. There's no authority in the Constitution for the federal government to be dealing with education. We should get rid of the loan programs. We should get rid of the Department of Education and give tax credits, if you have to, to help people.

Q: But how do they pay for it? How do they now pay for college?

PAUL: The way you pay for cellphones and computers. You have the marketplace there. There's competition. Quality goes up. The price goes down.

Source: 2011 CNBC GOP Primary debate in Rochester MI, Nov. 9, 2011

Obama on College Loans

$10K college tax credit; forgive loans for public service

In this economy, a high school diploma no longer guarantees a good job. That's why I urge the Senate to pass a bill that will revitalize our community colleges, which are a career pathway to the children of so many working families.

To make college more affordable, this bill will finally end the unwarranted taxpayer subsidies that go to banks for student loans. Instead, let's take that money and give families a $10,000 tax credit for four years of college & increase Pell Grants.

And let's tell another one million students that when they graduate, they will be required to pay only 10% of their income on student loans, and all of their debt will be forgiven after 20 years—and forgiven after 10 years if they choose a career in public service, because in the USA, no one should go broke because they chose to go to college.

And by the way, it's time for colleges and universities to get serious about cutting their own costs—because they, too, have a responsibility to help solve this problem.

Source: State of the Union Address, Jan. 27, 2010

Paul on Religious Values

School prayer is not a federal issue

[Limits on Constitutional authority] holds true for issues like prayer in schools. Such issues were never meant to be decided by federal judges. The whole point of the American Revolution was to vindicate the principle of local self government.

Source: The Revolution: A Manifesto, by Ron Paul, p. 61, April 1, 2008

Voted NO on allowing school prayer during the War on Terror

Children's Prayers Resolution: Expressing the sense of Congress that schools should allow children time to pray for, or silently reflect upon, the country during the war against terrorism.

Source: Bill sponsored by Rep. Isakson, R-GA; Bill H.Con.Res.239;
vote number 445 on Nov. 15, 2001

Obama on Religious Values

Listening to evangelicals bridges major political fault line

Today, white evangelical Christians are the heart and soul of the Republican Party's grassroots base. It is their issues—abortion, gay marriage, prayer in schools, intelligent design, Terri Schiavo, the posting of the Ten Commandments in the courthouse, home schooling, voucher plans, and the makeup of the Supreme Court—that often dominate the headlines and serve as one of the major fault lines in American politics. The single biggest gap in party affiliation is between those who attend church regularly and those who don't. Democrats, meanwhile, are scrambling to "get religion," even as a core segment of our constituency remains stubbornly secular, and fears that the agenda of an assertively Christian nation may not make room for them or their life choices.

The evangelists' success points to a hunger for the product they are selling, a hunger that goes beyond any particular issue or cause. They need an assurance that somebody out there cares about them, is listening to them.

Source: The Audacity of Hope, by Barack Obama, p.201-2, Oct. 1, 2006

Paul on Evolution

Evolution doesn't support atheism nor diminish God

The creationists frown on the evolutionists, and the evolutionists dismiss the creationists as kooky and unscientific. Lost in this struggle are those who look objectively at all the scientific evidence for evolution without feeling any need to reject the notion of an all-powerful, all-knowing Creator.

My personal view is that recognizing the validity of an evolutionary process does not support atheism nor should it diminish one's view about God and the universe. From my viewpoint, this is a debate about science and religion (and I wish it could be more civil!) and should not involve politicians at all.

Why can't this remain an academic debate and not be made the political issue it has become? The answer is simple. Both sides want to use the state to enforce their views on others. One side doesn't mind using force to expose others to prayer and professing their faith. The other side demands that they have the right never to be offended and demands prohibition of any public expression of faith.

Source: Liberty Defined, by Rep. Ron Paul, p.104–105, April 19, 2011

Obama on Evolution

Evolution & science
aren't incompatible with Christian faith

Q: If one of your daughters asked you, "Daddy, did God really create the world in 6 days?" What would you say?

A: What I believe is that God created the universe, and that the 6 days in the Bible may not be 6 days as we understand it. My belief is that the story that the Bible tells about God creating this magnificent Earth, that is fundamentally true. Now whether it happened exactly as we might understand it reading the text of the Bible, that I don't presume to know. But one last point—I do believe in evolution. I don't think that is incompatible with Christian faith. Just as I don't think science generally is incompatible with Christian faith. There are those who suggest that if you have a scientific bent of mind, then somehow you should reject religion. And I fundamentally disagree with that. In fact, the more I learn about the world, the more I know about science, the more I'm amazed about the mystery of this planet and this universe. And it strengthens my faith as opposed to weakens it.

Source: Democratic Compassion Forum at Messiah College,
April 13, 2008

Paul on School Vouchers

Competition helps, but vouchers
invite bureaucratic control

Competition is helpful in any endeavor. And this is true in education. The near monopoly control over the indoctrination of young people in our public school systems is counterbalanced by homeschooling, private schooling and education readily available on the Internet. The regulations on starting a variety of alternatives to public schooling are extremely tight and keep the market from operating as it might.

The effort to provide more competition to the public school system has not solved the problem, though there are always a few who benefit from vouchers, tax credits, and charter schools. Too often these efforts are unfairly made available and do not eliminate the power of the state to control the curriculum. The best interim option for reform would be to give a tax credit for all educational expenses. Vouchers invite bureaucratic control of their usage and are unfairly distributed.

Source: Liberty Defined, by Rep. Ron Paul, p. 78-79, April 19, 2011

Obama on School Vouchers

Vouchers don't solve the problems of our schools

McCAIN: I'm sure you're aware, Sen. Obama, of the program in the Washington, D.C., school system where vouchers are provided. It's a thousand and some 9,000 parents asked to be eligible for that.

OBAMA: The D.C. school system is in terrible shape, and it has been for a very long time. And we've got a wonderful new superintendent there who's working very hard with the young mayor.

McCAIN: Who supports vouchers.

OBAMA: Actually, she supports charters.

McCAIN: She supports vouchers, also.

OBAMA: Even if Sen. McCain were to say that vouchers were the way to go—I disagree with him on this, because the data doesn't show that it actually solves the problem—the centerpiece of Sen. McCain's education policy is to increase the voucher program in D.C. by 2,000 slots. That leaves all of you who live in the other 50 states without an education reform policy from Sen. McCain.

McCAIN: Because there's not enough vouchers; therefore, we shouldn't do it, even though it's working. I got it.

Source: Third presidential debate against John McCain, Oct. 15, 2008

Paul on Parental Leave

Voted NO on four weeks of paid parental leave for federal employees

Congressional Summary: Allows federal employees to substitute any available paid leave for any leave without pay available for either the: (1) birth of a child; or (2) placement of a child for either adoption or foster care. Makes available for any of the 12 weeks of leave an employee is entitled to for such purposes: (1) four weeks of paid parental leave in connection with the birth or placement involved; and (2) any accumulated annual or sick leave.

Proponent's argument to vote Yes: Rep. STEVE LYNCH (D, MA-9): This bill takes an important step toward improving the Federal Government's ability to recruit and retain a highly qualified workforce by providing paid parental leave to Federal and Congressional employees for the birth, adoption or placement of a child for foster care, which is a benefit that is extended to many in the private sector in other industrialized countries.

Opponent's argument to vote No: Rep. DARRELL ISSA (R, CA-49): This bill sends the wrong message at the wrong time to working American taxpayers and families that are struggling in difficult times. Our economy is in crisis, and deficits are already soaring. This bill does not have one provision to say if you make $170,000 a year, why do we have to give you this benefit? There are no safeguards at all. As a matter of fact, this bill envisions the $1 billion over 5 years, swelling to $4 billion over 10 years or more because, in fact, they believe it should be 8 weeks of special leave. Federal employees enjoy one of the highest levels of job security anywhere in the US. More importantly, in good times and bad, they keep their jobs.

Source: Federal Employees Paid Parental Leave Act; Bill H.R.626 ;
vote number H310 on June 4, 2009

Obama on Parental Leave

Help families with paid sick days and better family leave

Now is the time to help families with paid sick days and better family leave, because nobody in America should have to choose between keeping their jobs and caring for a sick child or ailing parent.

Source: Speech at 2008 Democratic National Convention, Aug. 27, 2008

Expand flex-work & Family and Medical Leave Act

Expand the Family and Medical Leave Act: The FMLA covers only certain workers in businesses with 50 or more employees. Obama will expand it to cover businesses with 25 or more employees. He will also include allowing workers to take leave for elder care needs; and to expand FMLA to cover leave for employees to address domestic violence.

Encourage States to Adopt Paid Leave: As president, Obama will initiate a strategy to encourage all 50 states to adopt paid-leave systems. Obama will provide a $1.5 billion fund to assist states with start-up costs.

Expand Flexible Work Arrangements: Obama will create a program to inform businesses about the benefits of flexible work schedules; help businesses create flexible work opportunities; and increase federal incentives for telecommuting. Obama will also make the federal government a model employer in terms of adopting flexible work schedules and permitting employees to request flexible arrangements.

Source: Campaign booklet, "Blueprint for Change," p. 10-15, Feb. 2, 2008

Paul on the Tea Party

Breaks one-day fundraising record:
$6M at "Boston Tea Party"

Ron Paul raised an astounding $6 million & change Sunday. The campaign announced they had eclipsed the $5.7 million that John Kerry raised the day after he locked up the 2004 Democratic nomination—arguably the largest single-day fundraising haul in US political history.

Paul, whose campaign has been embraced by a zealous community of online supporters, raised $4.2 million on Nov. 5, [corresponding with Guy Fawkes Day]. The current fundraising effort was timed for the 234th anniversary of the Boston Tea Party, a day meant to resonate with the Libertarian sensibilities of his supporters.

The man who engineered it—Trevor Lyman, a 37-year-old music promoter—has no official ties to the campaign and had no political experience before he engineered the innovative model for Nov. 5. He set up a website that solicited pledges for contributions to be made directly to the Paul campaign on that day—a technique that became known as a "money bomb," which he used again to such great effect Sunday.

Source: USA Today, Dec. 17, 2007

Obama on the Tea Party

92% of Tea Partiers:
"Obama is moving US toward socialism"

By April 2010, over half of the nation—and 92 percent of Tea Partiers—believed that President Obama was moving the country toward socialism. Combine our anxiety over the meltdown with today's downward economic mobility, and you get scapegoating run amok. A Harris Poll in March 2010 showed that, among Republicans, 57 percent believe Obama is a Muslim, 38 percent believe he "is doing many of the things that Hitler did," and 24 percent believe that the president "may be the Anti-Christ."

Source: Third World America, by Arianna Huffington, p. 86, Sept. 2, 2010

Paul on Principles of Liberty

Liberty promotes peace, and peace promotes prosperity

If you follow the Constitution, you will defend freedom. Freedom brings people together. It allows people to run their lives as they choose, it allows them to practice religion as they choose, it is not confrontational & not antagonistic. The welfare state, the warfare state, & the socialist state, is exactly the opposite. It divides us, because they take away our wealth, they control it in Washington.

What is happening today? Millions of dollars of campaign funds & PAC money, and lobbying efforts to control the money that gravitates to Washington, DC. The pie is shrinking, and the people are getting angry, and we have forgotten what a free country is all about.

We've lost our confidence, because we have to have safety nets here and safety nets here and do all of these things. It's coming to an end and there's a wonderful, beautiful answer. It comes in our traditions and it comes in the principles of liberty. If you promote liberty, liberty promotes peace. And peace promotes prosperity.

Source: Speeches to 2008 Conservative Political Action Conference,
Feb. 7, 2008

Obama on Principles of Liberty

No Obama Doctrine; just democracy, security, liberty

Obama's failure to condemn all military action has led to criticism from some on the left. One critic noted: "He accepts the Bush Doctrine. He accepts the doctrine of preemptive strikes."

The key part of the Bush Doctrine is the focus on unilateral action and the use of force to spread democracy around the world. And the worst part of the Bush administration is not the Bush Doctrine but Bush's implementation of it.

As Obama famously declared in 2002, he did not oppose all wars, but he did oppose a "dumb war." Isolationism must not be the reaction to a dumb president and a dumb war.

There is no Obama Doctrine because Obama is not a doctrinaire kind of leader who operates according to fixed policies. Instead, Obama believes in a set of principle (democracy, security, liberty) for the world and tries to come up with practical measures for incrementally increasing US security and global freedom. He rejects isolationism and he tries to steer clear of unilateralism.

Source: The Improbable Quest, by John K. Wilson, p.117–118,
Oct 30, 2007

Paul on Racism

Accused of racist remarks in 1980s newsletters

It's the biggest setback to hit Ron Paul's candidacy for president: publicity about racially charged statements and other controversial comments in newsletters published in Mr. Paul's name in the 1980s and 1990s. Paul responded by calling the newsletter statements "terrible" but insisting that he wasn't the one who wrote them. He added that the offensive comments totaled about "about eight or 10 sentences."

Some journalists who have researched the newsletters say it was a lot more than 10 sentences. The controversial statements that have surfaced stem largely from the period 1985 to 1994. Some samples: A Dec. 1989 newsletter predicted "Racial Violence Will Fill Our Cities" because "mostly black welfare recipients will feel justified in stealing from mostly white 'haves.'" Paul said he had "some moral responsibility" for the words [since the words appeared in his newsletters].

Source: Mark Trumbull in Christian Science Monitor, "Timeline"
Dec. 29, 2011

Obama on Racism

Speaks about racial anxiety from personal experience

Here is Obama casually sharing a reverie about race: "I imagine the white southerner who growing up heard his dad talk about niggers this & niggers that but who has struck up a friendship with the black guys at the office & is trying to teach his own son different, who thinks discrimination is wrong but doesn't see why the son of a black doctor should be admitted to law school ahead of his own son. Or the former Black Panther who decided to go into real estate, bought a few buildings in the neighborhood, & is just as tired of the drug dealers in front of those buildings as he is of the bankers who won't give him a loan to expand his business.

Deconstruct those two sentences. Yes, there is plenty of ugliness in America's racial history; blacks & whites alike have legitimate anxieties about race; redemption is always possible. This is a narrative that speaks to American life as it is lived. It conveys genuine empathy. It is intuitive Obama. No pollster or speechwriter could have composed that passage.

Source: Obama's Challenge, by Robert Kuttner, p. 8-9, Aug. 25, 2008

Paul vs. Obama
on International Issues

International issues focus on foreign relations and anything involving foreign nations, including the following topics:

- *Energy and Oil:* including global warming, domestic drilling and alternative energy sources. Rep. Paul focuses on avoiding international government and reducing federal government involvement. President Obama focuses on replacing oil.

- *Free Trade:* including NAFTA (the North American Free trade Agreement) and other bilateral agreements, plus opinions on the trade organizations like the WTO (World Trade Organization). Paul wants open trade with China; Obama agrees, but warily.

- *Immigration:* including border security; the border fence; and dealing with the current 12 million illegal immigrants in the US. Paul focuses on realistic methods of dealing with millions of illegal aliens; Obama focuses on avoiding anti-immigrant attitudes.

- *Foreign Policy:* Paul wants to reduce foreign aid and foreign entanglements. Obama believes in the United Nations and believes in talking with other countries, even our enemies.

- *Homeland Security:* this category concerns defense policy, not war policy. This category includes defense spending issues; and defense strategy goals. This is the oddest distinction between the two candidates: Paul wants dramatic decreases in defense spending; Obama wants an increase while ending the Iraq War.

- *War and Peace:* including the current ongoing wars in Iraq and Afghanistan. Obama has officially ended the Iraq War but maintains troops in Afghanistan, Kuwait, and elsewhere. Paul would withdraw from all foreign aggression.

Ron Paul
on International Issues

Barack Obama
on International Issues

Paul on Climate Change

Absurd to let global bureaucrats
try to manipulate climate

Regardless of whether one believes global warming is real, I seriously doubt the capacity of a global body made up of bureaucrats and scientists on the public payroll, when given the power to attempt a global climate manipulation, to cook up a workable plan with effects that cannot be discerned for twenty or more years. I've seen how government programs work. They aren't designed to last more than a single election cycle.

The idea that government can plan weather patterns for decades strikes me as the height of absurdity. Building up fear and manipulating people into demanding that government save is how radical environmentalists operate. Cap and trade legislation will introduce a whole new product of CO_2 permits that will be created and traded by the big financial interests bailed out after the crash, such as Goldman Sachs.

Source: Liberty Defined, by Rep. Ron Paul, p.133-136, April 19, 2011

NOTE: "Cap-and-Trade" refers to a carbon dioxide (CO_2) emissions policy where the amount of CO_2 is "capped" at a government-specified emission amount, and then the right to emit CO_2 is "traded" via emission permits. A similar program was used successfully to battle acid rain via sulfur dioxide emission permits trading on the Chicago Mercantile Exchange.

Obama on Climate Change

Aggressively address accelerating climate change

Q: What do you think the toughest choice you have left to make is?

A: The issue of climate change. I've put forward one of the most aggressive proposals out there, but the science seems to be coming in indicating it's accelerating even more quickly with every passing day. And by the time I take office, I think we're going to have to have a serious conversation about how drastic steps we need to take to address it.

Source: Democratic radio debate on NPR, Dec. 4, 2007

Cap-and-trade carbon emissions; raise CAFE standard

It's time to turn the page on energy, to break the stalemate that's kept our fuel efficiency standards in the same place for 20 years, to tell the oil and auto industries that they must act, not only because their future's at stake, but because the future of our country and our planet is at stake.

As president, I will place a cap on carbon emissions and require companies who can't meet the cap to buy credits from those who can, which will generate billions of dollars to invest in renewable sources of energy and create new jobs and even a new industry in the process. I'll put in place a low carbon fuel standard that will take 50 million cars worth of pollution off the road. I'll raise the fuel efficiency standards for our cars and trucks because we know we have the technology to do it and it's the time to do it.

Source: Take Back America 2007 Conference, June 19, 2007

Paul on Oil Drilling

Big Oil profits ok; Big Oil subsidies are not

Q: Bush's energy bill provided billions of dollars in tax breaks & subsidies to the oil companies with the goal of boosting domestic production at a time of record profits. Do you support that?

A: I don't think the profits is the issue. The profits are okay if they're legitimately earned in a free market. What I object to are subsidies to big corporations when we subsidize them and give them R&D money. I don't think that should be that way. They should take it out of the funds that they earn.

Source: 2007 GOP debate at Saint Anselm College, June 3, 2007

Obama on Oil Drilling

We cannot drill our way out of our addiction to oil

It is hard to overstate the degree to which our addiction to oil undermines our future. Without any change to energy policy, US demand for oil will jump 40% in 20 years. Over the same period, worldwide demand will jump 30%.

A large portion of the $800 million we spend on foreign oil every day goes to some of the world's most volatile regimes. And there are the environmental consequences. Just about every scientist outside the White House believes climate change is real.

We cannot drill our way out of the problem. Instead of subsidizing the oil industry, we should end every single tax break the industry currently receives and demand that 1% of the revenues from oil companies with over $1 billion in quarterly profits go toward financing alternative energy research and infrastructure.

Over the last 30 years, countries like Brazil have used a mix of regulation and direct government investment to develop a biofuel industry; 70% of its new vehicles run on sugar-based ethanol.

Source: The Audacity of Hope, by Barack Obama, p.167–169, Oct. 1, 2006

Paul on China Trade

China trade not contingent on human rights & product safety

Q: Sarah Lu was forced to work in labor camps for six years, for the crime of being a Christian house church leader. Thousands of prisoners of conscience are forced to manufacture items that stock our American shelves. Would you make future trade with China contingent on them measurably improving their record on religious freedom & human rights?

HUCKABEE: Yes.

TANCREDO: Yes.

COX: Yes.

BROWNBACK: Yes.

PAUL: No.

HUNTER: Absolutely. Yes. Good question.

KEYES: Yes.

Source: 2007 GOP Values Voter Presidential Debate, Sept. 17, 2007

Obama on China Trade

China is a competitor but not an enemy

Q: Given China's size, its muscular manufacturing capabilities, its military buildup, at this point—and also including its large trade deficit—at this point, who has more leverage, China or the U.S.?

A: Number one is we've got to get our own fiscal house in order. Number two, when I was visiting Africa, I was told by a group of businessmen that the presence of China is only exceeded by the absence of America in the entire African continent. Number three, we have to be tougher negotiators with China. They are not enemies, but they are competitors of ours. Right now the United States is still the dominant superpower in the world. But the next president can't be thinking about today; he or she also has to be thinking about 10 years from now, 20 years from now, 50 years from now.

Source: Des Moines Register Democratic debate, Dec. 13, 2007

U.S. needs to ameliorate trade relations with China

The U.S. should be firm on issues that divide us like Taiwan while flexible on issues that could unite us. We should insist on labor standards and human rights, the opening of Chinese markets fully to American goods, and the fulfillment of legal contracts with American businesses but without triggering a trade war as prolonged instability in the Chinese economy could have global economic consequences.

Source: In His Own Words, edited by Lisa Rogak, p. 22, March 27, 2007

Paul on Illegal Alien Deportation

No amnesty, but impractical to round up 12 million illegals

Q: Is it even practical to try to send 12 million illegal immigrants all home?

A: I would not sign a bill like [comprehensive immigration reform], because it would be amnesty. I also think that it's pretty impractical to get an army in this country to round up 12 or maybe 20 million. But I do believe that we have to stick to our guns on obeying the law, and anybody who comes in here illegally shouldn't be rewarded. And that would be the case.

Source: 2007 GOP Presidential Forum at Morgan State University,
Sep 27, 2007

No amnesty, but border fence isn't so important

Q: You voted to support that 700-mile fence along the border with Mexico. Is there a need for a similar fence along the border with Canada?

PAUL: No. The fence was my weakest reason for voting for that, but enforcing the law was important, and border security is important. And we've talked about amnesty, which I'm positively opposed to. If you subsidize something, you get more of it. We subsidize illegal immigration, we reward it by easy citizenship, either birthright or amnesty.

Source: 2007 GOP debate at Saint Anselm College, June 3, 2007

Obama on Illegal Alien Deportation

Stop expelling talented undocumented workers

I strongly believe that we should take on, once and for all, the issue of illegal immigration. And I am prepared to work with Republicans and Democrats to protect our borders, enforce our laws and address the millions of undocumented workers who are now living in the shadows. And let's stop expelling talented, responsible young people who could be staffing our research labs or starting a new business, who could be further enriching this nation.

Source: State of the Union speech, Jan. 25, 2011

Send 1,200 National Guard troops to southern border

President Obama is trying to create the impression of some activity to address border security. He announced that he will send 1,200 National Guard troops to the border, as a temporary measure, until an additional 1,000 Border Patrol agents are on the job. This has generated headlines—and I suppose it is better than the alternative of no additional troops or officers—but it is really a drop in the bucket. Consider that of those 1,200 troops, only 286 were assigned to Texas. The southern border of the United States stretches 1,954 miles, and 1,255 of them are in Texas. We have 60 percent of the border, yet less than 25 percent of the resources were given to Texas to deal with it. In the face of the soaring violence infesting our border communities as a result of the drug trade, this paltry effort is simply inviting more problems.

Source: Fed Up!, by Gov. Rick Perry, p.124, Nov. 15, 2010

Paul on Guest Workers

Give illegals limbo status: a green card with an asterisk

Immigrants who can't be sent back due to the magnitude of the problem should not be given citizenship—no amnesty should be granted. Maybe a "green card" with an asterisk could be issued. This in-between status, keeping illegal immigrants in limbo, will be said that it will create a class of 2nd-class citizens. Yet it could be argued that it may well allow some immigrants who come here illegally a beneficial status without automatic citizenship—a much better option than deportation.

Source: Liberty Defined, by Rep. Ron Paul, p.156, April 19, 2011

Voted YES on more immigrant visas for skilled workers

Vote to pass a bill to increase the number of temporary visas granted to highly skilled workers from 65,000 to 115,000 by the year 2000.

Source: Bill introduced by Smith, R-TX.; Bill HR 3736;
vote number 460 on Sept. 24, 1998

Obama on Guest Workers

Anti-immigrant bitterness stems from joblessness

Obama said at a private fund-raiser in San Francisco, "You go into some of the small towns in Pennsylvania, and like a lot of small towns in the Midwest, the jobs have been gone now for 25 years and nothing's replaced them. So it's not surprising then that [people there] get bitter, they cling to guns or religion or antipathy to people who aren't like them or anti-immigrant sentiment or anti-trade sentiment as a way to explain their frustrations."

Obama's "bitter/cling" comments seemed to [indicate] that he was, at bottom, a helpless and hopeless elitist.

Source: Game Change, by Heilemann & Halpern, p.240-241, Jan 11, 2010

Crack down on employers who hire illegal immigrants

Obama wants to remove incentives for illegals to enter the country by cracking down on employers who hire undocumented immigrants. Obama has championed a proposal to create a system so employers can verify that their employees are legally eligible to work in the US. Obama recognizes that immigration raids are ineffective, netting only 3,600 arrests in 2006.

Obama's priority is to stop the current illegal immigration into the United States, and then deal compassionately and fairly with the illegal immigrants who re already living here. If the flood of new immigrants can be slowed considerably, Obama believes that those currently living here, over time, can be effectively absorbed into the population and the economy.

Source: Obamanomics, by John R. Talbott, p.120-121, July 1, 2008

Paul on American Exceptionalism

Exceptionalism shouldn't mean using force around the world

There's been talk lately about American exceptionalism; it's been the greatest country, most freedom, most prosperity. My concern is I'm afraid we're losing it, I'm afraid we've given up on our devotion to liberty, that's where our problem is. But where I think we go astray on this exceptionalism is there are some people and sometimes they're referred as neoconservatives and they're sort of neo-Jacobins where they believe that we have this moral responsibility to use force to go around the world and say "you will do it our way or else." Well, force doesn't work; it never works.

The best way to get people to act more like us if we're doing a good job, is for us to have a sound economy, a sound dollar, treat people decently, have a foreign policy that makes common sense, treat people like we want to be treated, and then maybe they would want to emulate us and say "freedom does work and we ought to try it." But we can't force it on other people.

Source: Speech at 2011 Conservative Political Action Conference,
Feb 11, 2011

NOTE: "American exceptionalism" means that America has a unique status in the world today. The interest in American exceptionalism counters Obama's rejection of the concept, when Obama said, "Sure, I believe in American exceptionalism in the same way the British believe in British exceptionalism and the Greeks believe in Greek exceptionalism." Republicans generally interpret that as meaning, "No, I don't believe in your version of American exceptionalism at all."

Obama on American Exceptionalism

American exceptionalism is same as any other exceptionalism

Many people don't believe we have special message for the world or a special mission to preserve our greatness for the betterment of not just ourselves but all of humanity. Astonishingly, President Obama even said that he believes in American exceptionalism in the same way "the Brits believe in British exceptionalism and the Greeks believe in Greek exceptionalism." Which is to say, he doesn't believe in American exceptionalism at all. He seems to think it is just a kind of irrational prejudice in favor of our way of life. To me, that is appalling.

When President Obama insists that all countries are exceptional, he's saying that none is, last of all the country he leads. That's a shame, because American exceptionalism is something that people in both parties used to believe in.

Source: America by Heart, by Sarah Palin, p. 69, Nov. 23, 2010

Paul on North Korea

Get out of South Korea and let two Koreas unify

Q: Under President Paul, if North Korea invaded South Korea, would we respond?

A: Why should we unless the Congress declared war? I mean, why are we there? In South Korea, they're begging and pleading to unify their country, and we get in their way. They want to build bridges and go back and forth. Vietnam, we left under the worst of circumstances. The country is unified. They have become Westernized. We trade with them. Their president comes here. And Korea, we stayed there and look at the mess. I mean, the problem still exists, and it's drained trillion dollars over these last 50 years. We can't afford it anymore. We're going bankrupt. All empires end because the countries go bankrupt, and the currency crashes. That's what happening. And we need to come out of this sensibly rather than waiting for a financial crisis.

Source: Meet the Press: 2007 "Meet the Candidates" series,
Dec 23, 2007

Obama on North Korea

2007: Pledged to meet with leaders of Iran & North Korea

In a June 2007 debate, Obama unexpectedly pledged that, as president, he would willingly meet with the leaders of such rogue nations as Iran and North Korea without preconditions during his first term in office. "Well, I will not promise to meet with the leasers of these countries during my first year." Clinton interjected. "I don't want to be used for propaganda purposes. I don't want to make a situation even worse."

This looked like another Obama gaffe. The following day, Clinton's campaign recruited former secretary of state Madeleine Albright to lead the attack against Obama. During a telephone interview, she launched a personal attack on Obama, [saying], "I thought he was irresponsible and frankly naive."

Source: The Battle for America 2008, by Balz & Johnson, p. 83-84,
Aug 4, 2009

Engage North Korea in 6-party talks

[We should] address the threat posed by North Korea. By refusing to negotiate with North Korea for three and half years, experts believe that North Korea may now be close to having six to eight nuclear weapons. We must immediately insist on complete and verifiable elimination of North Korea's nuclear capability, engage in Six-Party bilateral talks, and facilitate a reform agenda that is broader than denuclearization to address humanitarian concerns.

Source: Press Release, "Renewal of American Leadership ," July 12, 2004

Paul on Iranian Sanctions

Israel won't attack Iran, and neither should we

Q: If Israel attacked Iran to prevent Tehran from getting nuclear weapons, would you help?

CAIN: If Israel had a credible plan that it appeared as if they could succeed, I would support Israel, yes.

PAUL: I wouldn't do that, because I don't expect it to happen. A Mossad leader said it would be the stupidest thing to do in the world. They're not about to do this. And you're supposing that if it did, why does Israel need our help? We need to get out of their way. When they want to have peace treaties, we tell them what they can do because we buy their allegiance and they sacrifice their sovereignty to us. And then they decide they want to bomb something, that's their business, but they should suffer the consequences. When they bombed the Iraqi nuclear site, back in the '80s, I was one of the few in Congress that said it's none of our business and Israel should take care of themselves. Why do we have this automatic commitment that we're going to send our kids and send our money endlessly to Israel?

Source: 2011 CNN National Security GOP primary debate Nov. 22, 2011

Obama on Iranian Sanctions

Iran is more isolated and will face growing consequences

Diplomatic efforts have strengthened our hand in dealing with those nations that insist on violating international agreements in pursuit of nuclear weapons. That's why North Korea now faces increased isolation, and stronger sanctions—sanctions that are being vigorously enforced. That's why the international community is more united, and the Islamic Republic of Iran is more isolated. And as Iran's leaders continue to ignore their obligations: They, too, will face growing consequences.

Source: State of the Union Address, Jan. 27, 2010

Must be tough on Iran, but talk to them too

Q: How big a threat is Iran to the US?

A: What we've seen over the last several years is Iran's influence grow. So our policy over the last eight years has not worked. We cannot tolerate a nuclear Iran. Not only would it threaten Israel, a country that is our stalwart ally, but it would also set off an arms race in the Middle East.

We are going to have to engage in tough direct diplomacy with Iran and this is a major difference I have with Senator McCain, this notion by not talking to people we are punishing them has not worked. It has not worked in Iran, it has not worked in North Korea. In each instance, our efforts of isolation have actually accelerated their efforts to get nuclear weapons.

Source: First presidential debate, Obama vs. McCain, Sept. 26, 2008

Paul on International Diplomacy

Right to spread our values, but wrong to spread by force

Q: President Bush said in his second inaugural address, "It is the policy of the US to seek and support the growth of democratic movements and institutions in every nation and culture." Has President Bush's policy been a success?

A: Our responsibility is to spread democracy here, make sure that we have it. This is a philosophic and foreign policy problem, because what the president was saying was just a continuation of Woodrow Wilson's "making the world safe for democracy." There's nothing wrong with spreading our values around the world, but it is wrong to spread it by force. We should spread it by setting an example and going and doing a good job here. Threatening Pakistan and threatening Iran makes no sense whatsoever. I supported going after Al Qaida into Afghanistan—but, lo & behold, the neocons took over. They forgot about Bin Laden. And what they did, they went into nation-building, not only in Afghanistan, they went unjustifiably over into Iraq. And that's why we're in this mess today.

Source: 2007 GOP Iowa Straw Poll debate, Aug. 5, 2007

Obama on International Diplomacy

The UN has succeeded in avoiding a Third World War

With the advent of the nuclear age, it became clear to victor and vanquished alike that the world needed institutions to prevent another World War. And so, a quarter century after the US Senate rejected the League of Nations—an idea for which Woodrow Wilson received this Prize—America led the world in constructing an architecture to keep the peace: a Marshall Plan and a United Nations, mechanisms to govern the waging of war, treaties to protect human rights, prevent genocide, and restrict the most dangerous weapons.

In many ways, these efforts succeeded. Yes, terrible wars have been fought, and atrocities committed. But there has been no Third World War. The Cold War ended with jubilant crowds dismantling a wall. Billions have been lifted from poverty. The ideals of liberty, self-determination, equality and the rule of law have haltingly advanced. We are the heirs of the fortitude and foresight of generations past, and it is a legacy for which my own country is rightfully proud.

Source: Nobel Peace Prize acceptance speech in Oslo, Norway,
Dec 10, 2009

Paul on Foreign Aid

Foreign aid wastes billions, with unintended consequences

Believing foreign aid benefits our national security allows for billions of dollars to be wasted, encouraging a foreign policy that inevitably leads to unintended consequences that come back to haunt us. Foreign aid support comes for various reasons. Some argue we are obligated to financially support those countries that yield to our demand that we maintain military bases in their country.

American citizens are taxed to fund these foreign giveaway programs. That means funds are taken out of the hands of private citizens. Allowing government or bureaucratic decisions on spending capital is always inferior to private companies and people deciding how the money should be spent. But most importantly, foreign aid never works to achieve the stated goal of helping the poor of other nations. In poor countries food aid becomes a tool for maintaining political power. Many of the large foreign aid grants are driven strictly by special interest politics and a pretense that it serves our national security.

Source: Liberty Defined, by Rep. Ron Paul, p.118-119, April 19, 2011

Obama on Foreign Aid

Global Poverty Act: spend 0.7% of GDP on foreign aid

As the Democratic primaries were winding down in May 2008, Obama quietly steered his Global Poverty Act, known as S. 2433, through the Senate. Obama likes to characterize S. 2433 as requiring "the president to develop and implement a comprehensive policy to cut extreme global poverty in half by 2015 through aid, trade debt relief, and coordination with the international community, businesses and NGOs (non-governmental organizations)." Obama clearly hopes he will be in his second term as president by then, so reduction of global poverty by half can be tracked back to his co-sponsorship of this visionary piece of legislation.

Critics on the right, who were anything but enthusiastic, sarcastically renamed the bill the "Global Poverty Tax." The legislation "would commit the U.S. to spending 0.7 percent of Gross Domestic Product on foreign aid, which amounts to a phenomenal total of $845 billion over and above what the U.S. already spends.

Source: Obama Nation, by Jerome Corsi, p.250, Aug. 1, 2008

Paul on the Patriot Act

The Patriot Act is unpatriotic; it undermines our liberty

OBAMA: [to Paul]: I would not change the PATRIOT Act. And I'd look at strengthening it, because I think the dangers are literally that great.

PAUL: I think the Patriot Act is unpatriotic because it undermines our liberty. I'm concerned, as everybody is, about the terrorist attack. Timothy McVeigh was a vicious terrorist. He was arrested. Terrorism is still on the books, internationally and nationally, it's a crime and we should deal with it. We dealt with it rather well with McVeigh.

OBAMA: Timothy McVeigh succeeded. That's the whole point.

PAUL: Why I really fear it is we have drifted into a condition that we were warned against because our early founders were very clear. They said, don't be willing to sacrifice liberty for security. Today it seems too easy that our government is so willing to give up our liberties for security. I have a personal belief that you never have to give up liberty for security. You can still provide security without sacrificing our Bill of Rights.

Source: 2011 CNN National Security GOP primary debate, Nov. 22, 2011

Obama on the Patriot Act

The politics of fear undermines basic civil liberties

What we cannot continue to do is operate as if we are the weakest nation in the world instead of the strongest one, because that's not who we are and that's not what the US has been about, historically. It is starting to warp our domestic policies, as well. We haven't even talked about civil liberties and the impact of that politics of fear—what that has done to us, in terms of undermining basic civil liberties in this country, what it has done in terms of our reputation around the world.

Source: Democratic debate at Drexel University, Oct. 30, 2007

FactCheck: Promised to repeal Patriot Act, then voted for it

Clinton took direct aim at Obama and connects fairly solidly: "You said you would vote against the Patriot Act; you came to the Senate, you voted for it." Clinton is correct to say that Obama opposed the Patriot Act during his run for the Senate. When it came time to reauthorize the law in 2005, though, Obama voted in favor of it. He started out opposing it: In Dec. 2005, Obama voted against ending debate—a position equivalent to declaring a lack of support for the measure. Then in February of that year, Obama said on the floor that he would support the Patriot Act's reauthorization. In March 2006, Obama both voted for cloture and for the Patriot Act reauthorization conference report. Clinton, by the way, followed exactly the same path on the 2005 bill, from speaking in opposition to voting for it.

Source: FactCheck.org on Facebook/WMUR-NH Democratic debate,
Jan. 5, 2008

Paul on Defense spending

We can blow up the world 20 times and we can't cut a penny?

Sen. RICK SANTORUM: [to Paul]: I would absolutely not cut one penny out of military spending. We should have all the resources in place to make sure that we can defend our borders, that we can make sure that when we engage in foreign countries, we do so to succeed. The central threat right now is Iran.

PAUL: Well, I think we're on economic suicide if we're not even willing to look at some of these overseas expenditures, 900 bases, 150 different countries. We have enough weapons to blow up the world about 20-25 times. We have more weapons than all the other countries put together essentially. And we want to spend more and more, and you can't cut a penny? I mean, this is why we're at an impasse. I want to hear somebody up here willing to cut something. Something real. This budget is in bad shape and the financial calamity is going to be much worse than anybody ever invading this country. Which country is going to invade this country? They can't even shoot a missile at us.

Source: GOP 2011 primary debate in Las Vegas, Oct. 18, 2011

Obama on Defense spending

Grow size of military to maintain rotation schedules

Our most complex military challenge will involve putting boots on the ground in the ungoverned or hostile regions where terrorists thrive. That requires a smarter balance between what we spend on fancy hardware and what we spend on our men and women in uniform. That should mean growing the size of our armed forces to maintain reasonable rotation schedules, keeping our troops properly equipped, and training them in the skills they'll need to succeed in increasingly complex and difficult missions.

Source: The Audacity of Hope, by Barack Obama, p.307, Oct. 1, 2006

Give our soldiers the best equipment and training available

[The US should] prepare our military to meet the new threats of the 21st century. We must prepare our military to meet the new threats of the 21st century by making sure that we have sufficient forces and by giving our soldiers the best equipment and training available. We must also ensure that members of our National Guard and reservists have access to affordable, quality health care.

Source: Press Release, "Renewal of American Leadership ," July 12, 2004

Paul on Sources of Terrorism

We believe Osama's threats,
so why not believe his reasons?

We believe bin Laden when he takes credit for an attack on the West, & we believe him when he warns us of an impending attack. But we refuse to listen to his explanations of why he & his allies are at war with us.

Bin Laden's claims are straightforward The US defiles Islam with military bases on holy land in Saudi Arabia, its initiation of war against Iraq, and its dollars and weapons being used against the Palestinians as the Palestinian territory shrinks and Israel's occupation expands. There will be no peace for the next 50 years or longer if we refuse to believe why those who are attacking are doing it.

To dismiss terrorism as the result of Muslims hating us because we're free is one of the greatest foreign-policy frauds ever perpetuated. Because the media and government have restated it so many times, the majority now accept it at face value. And the administration gets the political cover it needs to pursue a holy war for democracy against the infidels who hate us for our goodness.

Source: House speech, in Foreign Policy of Freedom, p.246, Jan. 29, 2003

Obama on Sources of Terrorism

Battling terrorism must go beyond belligerence vs. isolation

We know that the battle against terrorism is at once an armed struggle and a contest of ideas, that our long-term security depends on a judicious projection of military power and increased cooperation with other nations, and that addressing the problems of global poverty and failed states is vital to our nation's interests rather than just a matter of charity. But follow most of our foreign policy debates, and you might believe that we have only two choices—belligerence or isolationism.

Source: The Audacity of Hope, by Barack Obama, p. 23, Oct. 1, 2006

OpEd: Claims "poverty causes terrorism" but they're educated

Most suicide bombers are well-educated and have a generally higher socio-economic status. Nevertheless, the Obama administration continues to cling to the "poverty causes terrorism" theory because it supports the social work approach to national security that it favors.

If the Obama administration were to admit that Islamic terrorists are not motivated by poverty but rather by an evil ideology, that would require a paradigm shift in the way it approaches terrorism. They'd have to name the enemy, and acknowledge that military power rather than more anti-poverty programs must be the central means to fight and win.

Source: Leadership and Crisis, by Bobby Jindal, p.257-258, Nov. 15, 2010

Paul on Iraq War

The Iraq war was not worth the price
in blood and treasure

Q: Was the war a good idea and worth the price in blood and treasure?

A: It was a very bad idea, and it wasn't worth it. The al Qaeda wasn't there then; they're there now. There were no weapons of mass destruction. Had nothing to do with 9/11. There was no aggression. This decision on policy was made in 1998 because they called for the removal of Saddam Hussein. It wasn't worth it, and it's a sad story because we started that war and we should never be a country that starts war needlessly.

Source: 2008 GOP debate in Boca Raton Florida, Jan. 24, 2008

War in Iraq was senseless invasion of sovereign state

The war in Iraq was one of the most ill-considered, poorly planned and just plain unnecessary military conflicts in American history, and I opposed it from the beginning.

Source: The Revolution: A Manifesto, by Ron Paul, p. 21, April 1, 2008

Obama on Iraq War

Iraq has distracted us from Taliban in Afghanistan

Afghanistan is an area where we should be focusing. NATO has made real contributions there. Unfortunately, because of the distraction of Iraq, we have not finished the job in terms of making certain that we are driving back the Taliban, stabilizing the Karzai government, capturing bin Laden and making sure that we've rooted out terrorism in that region.

Source: South Carolina Democratic primary debate, on MSNBC,
Apr 26, 2007

Iraq: 100,000 troops have left; let's finish the job

Look to Iraq, where nearly 100,000 of our brave men and women have left with their heads held high. American combat patrols have ended, violence is down, and a new government has been formed. This year, our civilians will forge a lasting partnership with the Iraqi people, while we finish the job of bringing our troops out of Iraq. America's commitment has been kept. The Iraq war is coming to an end.

Source: State of the Union speech, Jan. 25, 2011

Note: The Iraq War formally ended on Dec. 15, 2011. Approximately 5,000 "security contractors" will remain to guard the US Embassy in Baghdad, plus several thousand more "general support contractors." Another 9,000 US troops are just over the border in Kuwait.

Paul on Torture Policy

Waterboarding is torture:
illegal, uncivilized, and immoral

Q: Does waterboarding constitute torture?

CAIN: I don't see it as torture. I would return to that policy.

PAUL: Waterboarding is torture. It's illegal under international law and under our law. It's also immoral. And it's also impractical. There's no evidence that you really get reliable evidence. Why would you accept the position of torturing 100 people because you know one person might have information? And that's what you do when you accept the principal of torture. I think it's uncivilized and has no practical advantages and is really un-American to accept on principal that we will torture people that we capture.

Source: Debate in South Carolina on Foreign Policy, Nov. 12, 2011

100 detainees have died of torture under US custody

The image of Americans torturing prisoners at Abu Ghraib and Guantanamo circulated around the Muslim world has done unbelievable harm by the hatred it generated against all Americans. It's going to take a lot of time to alter that sentiment, and it won't happen without a change in our foreign policy and our assumption that we can arrest anybody anywhere in the world at will. The ACLU and many news sources estimate that at least 100 detainees died as a result of torture while in American custody. Our government has tried to downplay those deaths as suicide. There's been no effort to hold accountable the individuals responsible for this travesty.

Source: Liberty Defined, by Rep. Ron Paul, p.293–294, April 19, 2011

Obama on Torture Policy

No torture; no renditions; no operating out of fear

We have to be clear and unequivocal. We do not torture, period. Our government does not torture. That should be our position. That will be my position as president. That includes renditions. We don't farm out torture. We don't subcontract torture. Torture does not end up yielding good information—most intelligence officers agree with that—but it is also important for our long-term security to send a message to the world that we will lead not just with our military might but we are going to lead with our values and our ideals. That we are not a nation that gives away our civil liberties simply because we're scared. We're always at our worst when we're fearful. Fear is a bad counsel and I want to operate out of hope and out of faith.

Source: Democratic Compassion Forum at Messiah College, April 13, 2008

Congress decides what constitutes torture, not president

Q: If Congress prohibits a specific interrogation technique, can the president instruct his subordinates to employ that technique despite the statute?

A: No. The President is not above the law, and not entitled to use techniques that Congress has specifically banned as torture. We must send a message to the world that America is a nation of laws, and a nation that stands against torture. As President I will abide by statutory prohibitions for all US Government personnel and contractors.

Source: Boston Globe questionnaire on Executive Power, Dec. 20, 2007

Book Reviews

OnTheIssues excerpts political books and debates as the primary source of the materials in this book. Following are several book reviews, plus links online to additional books and debates cited in this book.

Book reviews:

Additional book excerpts online:

Game Change, by Heilemann and Halperin (2010)
    www.OnTheIssues.org/Game_Change.htm

End the Fed, by Ron Paul (2010)
    www.OnTheIssues.org/*End_Fed*.htm

What Obama Means, by Jabari Asim (2009)
    www.OnTheIssues.org/Obama_Means.htm

The Faith of Barack Obama, by Stephen Mansfield (2008)
    www.OnTheIssues.org/*Faith_Obama.htm*

Gold, Peace, and Prosperity, by Ron Paul (2007)
    www.OnTheIssues.org/Gold_Peace.htm

A Foreign Policy of Freedom, by Ron Paul (2001)
    www.OnTheIssues.org/Foreign_Freedom.htm

Book Review: Liberty Defined:
50 Essential Issues
That Affect Our Freedom
by Rep. Ron Paul (April 19, 2011)

This book is Ron Paul's attempt to communicate libertarian ideas to his large group of followers, many of whom are new to libertarianism. It catalogs key concepts in alphabetical order, with a few pages dedicated to everything from Abortion to Zionism. Presumably the intent is that Paul's followers have a handy reference in which to look up his views, and the general libertarian view, on key issues of the 2012 presidential race.

Rep. Paul describes the book in the introduction: "The idea of this book is not to provide a blueprint for the future or an all-encompassing defense of a libertarian program. What I offer here are... not final answers but rather guideposts for thinking seriously about these topics." (p. xvii)

Paul extends in this book beyond the typical policy prescriptions about current issues and into libertarian philosophy and history. OnTheIssues covers the current issues in our excerpts below, so we'll review here some of the books' philosophical topics, which include:

Austrian Economics: A review of the 19th century philosophy underlying much of today's free-market economic outlook.

Demagogues: The bad guys in the bipartisanship debate, focusing on the "despicable" Pledge of Allegiance and flag-burning issues rampant among Republican demagogues. There's also a chapter on bipartisanship, which Paul doesn't like (a failure of bipartisanship means fewer bad laws).

Empire: Rep. Paul outlines the dangers of military over-extension from the Roman Empire and connects that to the current American Empire. Throughout the book, Rep. Paul tosses in statistics about American imperialism and world-wide militarism (another of his big differentiators from mainstream Republicans) such as "Wars and exterminations in the 20th century reached 262 million people killed by their own governments" (p. 107)

Keynesianism: This is the philosophical opposite of Austrian Economics, and is the current underlying philosophy of Bush's & Obama's economic stimulus package,

Noble Lie: How politicians justify doing whatever they want, by claiming it's good for the country. George W. Bush's advisers fall heavily under this rubric, following Adolf Hitler and others. Julian Assange, the founder of WikiLeaks, is the hero of this chapter, since he exposed the Noble Lies of the U.S. government.

The book was written in anticipation of Rep. Paul's entry into the presidential race, released in early 2011. Paul was the Internet darling of the 2008 race, and the 2012 race is shaping up with the same following. That means thousands of young people will discover Ron Paul and will read this book for a fuller introduction to libertarianism. The approach is self-standing essays of just-a-few-pages-at-a-time, instead of a fully-involved book.

Ron Paul has plenty of fully-involved books for when his followers want yet more (as they always do). For the hardier Paulista, *End the Fed*, published in 2010, provides substantially more detail about the Federal Reserve and the economic situation.

Book review written Aug. 2011;
full excerpts available online at:
www.ontheissues.org/Liberty_Defined.htm

Book Review:
Dreams from My Father:
A Story of Race and Inheritance
by Barack Obama (August 1996)

This is the book to read if you want to understand Obama's personal background and how it forms his character. It was written while he was still only an obscure State Senator—written in his spare time, without a ghost writer, while struggling to make ends meet on a state senator's salary. Therefore it is an honest portrait, made before Obama even intended to run for US Senate, much less for President.

Here I'll discuss one aspect of Obama's background, which is his internationalism. I'm writing this shortly after Obama returned from his "campaign trip" abroad, which included fact-finding in Iraq and drawing a crowd of 200,000 fans in Germany. While the mainstream press was overwhelmingly enamored with Obama on that trip, it has become clear upon Obama's return that the voting public has not responded nearly as positively. Obama's popularity abroad relates to Obama's international upbringing, as outlined in this book.

Obama spent several years of his childhood living abroad—four years in Indonesia. In addition, he maintains contact with his paternal family in Kenya (where, during his 2007 visit, he also was greeted as a hero). And his birthplace and family home is Hawaii, arguably the most international of the fifty states.

The question for the presidential race is this: Does Obama's personal experience living abroad count as foreign policy expertise? I would say Yes; but the voting public has declared No. In other words, McCain's argument that Obama has no foreign policy expertise has prevailed.

I would say Yes, because I personally have a similar experience as Obama, and I consider that a valid basis for claiming foreign policy expertise. I've resided in Denmark, Hong Kong, and Israel, for 6 to 12 months each; I've traveled to more than 40 countries and spent a total of about 4 or 5 years abroad; I've been in relationships with women living in England, Denmark, Hong Kong, and Pakistan. I do consider that I have substantial foreign policy expertise, entirely on the basis of that personal experience.

To illustrate why that qualifies me as a foreign policy expert, I'll relate my experience in a class on foreign policy at the Master's degree level at Harvard University in the early 1990s. I attended an introductory class on foreign policy with the intent of concentrating in that field. But I found that my fellow students had relatively little knowledge of world politics—despite that most had just graduated from foreign policy undergraduate institutions. For example, we discussed Japan's relations with its neighbors, and my fellow students suggested that Japan should be creating a trading bloc (like ASEAN or NAFTA) with China, Korea, and Russia, its nearest neighbors. It was obvious to me that Japan could never do such a thing, because the Koreans await an apology for WWII enslavement; the Chinese await reparations for the "Rape of Nanjing"; and the Russians await resolution of the disputed Kuril Islands. I knew those things first-hand from Japanese co-workers in Hong Kong, who were reluctant to visit those areas with me. My classmates knew little about those sort of "facts on the ground," and I ended up switching my field of concentration to the more experience-oriented "International Development."

Obama is an internationalist. That means, not only does he believe in globalization as an economic and military policy, but he is accustomed to presenting himself abroad as an American—which most Americans are not. America is an isolated country—unless we go out of our way to travel abroad and experience it intimately, we don't participate in the rest of the world. The consequence of that isolation is that we don't deeply understand foreigners' points of view. Internationalist Americans DO understand foreigners—and foreigners are well-aware of distinguishing internationalist Americans from our more isolated brethren. Obama's massive crowd of supporters in Germany was an acknowledgement from the Germans that they recognize Obama as an internationalist. The press' enthrallment with Obama on his foreign trip was because the press saw that other foreigners recognized that too, and assumed it would translate to popularity at home.

But most Americans are not internationalists. The press got it wrong because they only reported on what foreigners felt—while foreigners don't vote in the US presidential election. Obama thought he would be seen on this trip as Presidential—but in fact his popularity abroad was seen as just another way in which Obama differs from most Americans, because most Americans are not internationalist. Hence Obama's trip abroad was seen as elitist by most American voters—not as evidence of foreign policy expertise, even though it *WAS* seen that way abroad.

I consider myself an internationalist too. But I acknowledge that I'm in a small minority among my countrymen. My internationalist background certainly colors all of my politics—but usually I shut up about the origins of my political philosophy, because I don't want to be seen as elitist.

How does all that affect the presidential election? Well, Obama better shut up about his internationalism too, or he'll alienate most Americans by seeming elitist. And, although any internationalist would certainly grant Obama the lead over McCain in relevant foreign policy expertise, the American voting public will not. Therefore Obama needs to pick a Vice President who has more conventional foreign policy expertise, to counter McCain's attacks on this front.

Book review written Aug. 2008;
full excerpts available online at:
www.ontheissues.org/Dreams_From_My_Father.htm

Book Review:
Freedom Under Siege:
The US Constitution
After 200-Plus Years
by Rep. Ron Paul
(first published 1987;
reprinted Nov. 2007)

This book was written in 1987 and re-released for Paul's presidential campaign in 2007. It has no 2007 update, unfortunately, so we have to infer that Rep. Paul still subscribes to all of his policy prescriptions from 20 years ago.

The theme of this book is that big government is reducing our personal freedom, slowing our economy, and ultimately will destroy the country.

This book will be of interest to people who want a deeper understanding of what libertarians are talking about, and why Rep. Paul has generated such a large army of "Paulistas" in his presidential campaign. Rep. Paul's libertarian philosophy is well-documented here, although he would prefer the term "constitutionalist," meaning one who strictly follows the Constitution.

The book consists of four chapters:

- *Individual Rights:* This topic spans topics from morality to gun control, and we excerpt it heavily. Rep. Paul's thesis is: follow the Constitution, or follow the Amendment process if you don't like what's in the Constitution.

- *Foreign Policy:* This topic is covered in more detail in Paul's 2007 book, A Foreign Policy of Freedom. We excerpt it heavily to contrast to Rep. Paul's current statements on Iraq (anyone who knows Rep. Paul's level of consistency on this topic will know that by "compare" we mean "substantiate that he has indeed held the same views for 20 years now.")

- **The Military Draft:** This topic seems very outdated now, so we include just one representative excerpt. Rep. Paul makes only passing reference to the concept of "National Service," which would be the modern equivalent of this topic.

- **Sound Money is Gold:** This topic is covered in more detail in Rep. Paul's 1981 book, Gold, Peace, and Prosperity. We include a couple of excerpts and refer more interested readers to that source.

Book review written Dec. 2007;
full excerpts available online at:
www.ontheissues.org/Freedom_Under_Siege.htm

Book Review:
The Revolution:
A Manifesto
by Rep. Ron Paul (April 1, 2008)

This book is as close as Ron Paul's 2008 campaign gets to a campaign book. It was published in April 2008, amid Ron Paul's presidential primary campaign, and the title refers to the "Ron Paul Revolution" using the term that his supporters coined.

This book outlines Rep. Paul's general stances on the issues, both political and policy. Paul's policies are more libertarian than conservative—he opposes all government intervention, including the Iraq War. Paul clarifies here how he's often anti-Republican—bashing the GOP "Contract with America" as well as Bush's signing statements. But he is a Republican—pro-life and anti-foreign aid.

The title term "Revolution" refers to the grassroots campaign's self-described "Ron Paul Revolution." Their most substantive claim to a revolution is in how Paul's grassroots supporters—independent of the formal campaign—organized a pair of fundraising events in late 2007 that set fundraising records. The first event, on Nov. 5, a historic date known as Guy Fawkes Day, raised $4.2 million; the second event, on the anniversary of the Boston Tea Party, broke that record again.

The events were organized primarily on the internet, and while the campaign was aware of the "money bombs," the campaign itself did not organize the events. Howard Dean supporters will recognize that the techniques they pioneered in 2004 were used to great effect by Ron Paul supporters. While the Deanies in 2004 had to contend with defining FEC 527 laws and independent grassroots fundraising, the Paulistas in 2008 knew all the rules in advance. Both campaigns will presumably be used as models for future grassroots fundraising.

Paul has several more detailed books for those interested in a deeper dive into libertarian policy. The three that we've excerpted are Paul's book on foreign policy, *A Foreign Policy of Freedom*; on economics, *Gold, Peace, and Prosperity*; and on Constitutional issues, *Freedom Under Siege*. Those three books were written well before the presidential campaign, but have been more recently updated in some parts.

Book review written Nov. 2008;
full excerpts available online at:
www.ontheissues.org/Revolution_Manifesto.htm

Book Review:
The Audacity of Hope:
Thoughts on Reclaiming
the American Dream
by Barack Obama (Oct. 2006)

Who is the audience for this book? Most people buy it to keep it on their coffeetable to start conversations—the typical voter would not read it through. Most political analysts know everything that's in here already—there are no daring new policies nor deep personal revelations. I've concluded that the intended audience is the excerpter—people like me. This book got excerpted in Time magazine, for example, and Obama got a big cover spread, with a presidential headline. The Time excerpts were pleasant to read—a little uplift for a few pages. But the book is just so chock-full of respectfulness and understanding and consensus-building and bipartisanship that no excerpter can find anything *but* uplift in any excerpt (including me).

So my conclusion is that the book is *intended* for that purpose—a successful attempt to get Obama into the national spotlight by writing a political tome that everyone will like and few will actually read through. This book contains nothing but numerous uplifting anecdotes of building consensus based on understanding one's opponents' point of view, of bipartisanship based on mutual respect. Reading an excerpt or two fills one with an uplifting feeling. Reading the original in its entirety, however, feels like slogging through uplifting anecdote after uplifting anecdote, to the point where it feels formulaically forced. The formula goes like this for every issue: "The proponents believe X. The opponents believe Y. I tend to lean toward the proponents' views, but I have great respect for the opponents, and we should work together on consensus solutions." I imagine that Obama met with his ghostwriter and outlined his issue stances, then told the ghostwriter to frame each one in a context of that sort of bipartisan respect.

Overall, of course, this is exactly the sort of book needed for the presidential trail. Having the book on coffeetables across America, despite being unread, means Barack's smiling face is in people's living rooms and he's in people's conversations. Having uplifting anecdotes excerpted in Time and OnTheIssues means people will read about their favorite topic, be uplifted, and repeat the anecdote to their fellow voters. It doesn't matter that the *same* formula is used for *every* issue—people aren't interested in *every* issue, just their favorite ones. But if you want to get to know Obama, read instead Dreams From My Father, which is indeed a revealing biography and a deep look at his compelling personal story. This book is written instead for the campaign trail.

I do have a fantasy about how Obama came up with the title (because people like Obama hire people like me to come up with titles like "The Audacity of Hope"). I imagine that Obama wants to elicit a subconscious connection with Howard Dean—who is characterized by his audacious campaign style—and simultaneously elicit a subconscious connection with Bill Clinton—whose book titles often include his hometown of Hope, Arkansas, as in *Between Hope and History*. Obama's title hence attempts to elicit a subconscious feeling that "Obama has the audacity of Dean, but with Clinton's chances of success." Maybe I'm reading too much subconsciousness into it—but it's people like me who write these titles, so who knows.

Summer 2008 postscript: Indeed my title theory was a fantasy— the title came from a sermon given by the now-famous Rev. Jeremiah Wright.

Book review written May 2007;
full excerpts available online at:
www.ontheissues.org/Audacity_of_Hope.htm

Book Review:
Obama's Challenge:
America's Economic Crisis and the
Power of a Transformative Presidency,
by Robert Kuttner (Aug. 25, 2008)

We expected this book to be a perceptive analysis of the Obama campaign, since it won a prize (the Sidney Hillman Award), and since the author, Robert Kuttner, co-founded "The American Prospect," a well-respected liberal publication. Alas, the author is partisan rather than perceptive, and the book is fatally tainted by the author's biases. Some partisanship, and some punditry, are forgivable. But the fatal taint comes from the unforgivable—and politically inaccurate— partisanship of mischaracterizing "progressives" vs. "liberals."

Kuttner can be forgiven for some partisanship, since he's a well-known as a liberal Democrat. Perceptive readers recognize his partisanship in his statement describing Obama's activist use of government: "Which party is more likely to manage government in a way that doesn't arbitrarily diminish rights?" (p. 90). Well, which rights? Kuttner means gay rights, civil rights, labor rights, and so on. But a conservative could answer, "The GOP, of course, is less likely to diminish gun rights, free trade rights, and the right to life." After statements like Kuttner's above, readers acknowledge that Kuttner is writing an opinion piece, not an analysis piece, and thereafter read the book cautiously, differentiating Kuttner's opinions from analysis about Obama.

Kuttner can also be forgiven for some punditry, since he has earned his place as a pundit. He wrote this book during the 2008 election, and published it in August 2008, as "a citizen's open letter" to the Obama campaign. Kuttner admits his presumptuousness in predicting that Obama will win the election three months hence; readers acknowledge Kuttner's presumptuousness in thinking that the Obama campaign would care about his "open letter." After all, it's also an "open letter" to his fellow citizens, about how Obama would be a "transformative president" (that's Kuttner's subtitle. He means Obama will permanently change America, as did Abraham Lincoln, FDR, and Ronald Reagan).

But Kuttner cannot be forgiven for mischaracterizing the term "progressive." That term defined the difference between Obama (a progressive) and Hillary Clinton (a liberal) during the 2008 primary, so it is core to the election. Kuttner does identify Obama as a progressive, but also identifies as progressives LBJ, Hillary, John Edwards, and others. Kuttner writes in chapter one, "Progressives who backed Obama rather than John Edwards or Hillary Clinton for the Democratic nomination gave Obama a pass on some of the issues." (pp. 7-8). That statement is politically inaccurate twice. Where I come from, no progressives backed John Edwards nor Hillary Clinton. I know many, many progressives—they all backed Obama, or Dennis Kucinich, or maybe Mike Gravel. And I know many, many liberals—they all backed John Edwards or Hillary Clinton. It was a clean split, where I come from—and that's also where Kuttner comes from, since we both live in the Boston area. Kuttner must be well-aware of that split, but he misleads his readers by conflating the two political philosophies.

The second inaccuracy in that same statement is that progressives gave Obama a pass on some issues. Kuttner thinks like a liberal, and that statement only makes sense from a liberal perspective, where the focus is on economic issues (labor rights, appropriate taxation, protecting Social Security). Progressives instead focus on social issues (gay rights, protesting and ending the Iraq war, civil rights). Progressives backed Obama because he matched their views and their focus on social issues; liberals backed Hillary and Edwards on the same grounds for economic issues. Progressives would not give a pass to Hillary or Edwards for their pro-Iraq war votes because that's a core part of the progressive agenda.

That distinction between economic issues and social issues is the focal distinction of this website—see our "VoteMatch Quiz" for details. That same distinction differentiated Obama from Hillary, and differentiates the two factions of the Democratic Party, the progressives vs. the liberals. And that same distinction applies to the Republican

Party too—its current three factions differ in their social vs. economic focus:

- Christian conservatives focus on social issues (on the opposite side from progressives)

- Tea Party conservatives focus on economic issues (on the opposite side from liberals)

- Libertarians focus on both issues at once (on the opposite side from populists, but these groups aren't relevant to this discussion).

Kuttner's truly unforgivable partisanship comes from mischaracterizing the 2006 Senate election. This statement goes beyond partisan punditry into the realm of factual misrepresentation: "All six of the Democrats who took back Republican senate seats in 2006 ran as resolute progressives." (p. 112) Huh?!? Let's take a look at the six Democrats Kuttner refers to:

- Sherrod Brown (D, OH) and Sheldon Whitehouse (D, RI) are indeed resolute progressives.

- Claire McCaskill (D, MO) is best described as a moderate, not a "resolute progressive," but the other three should not even be described as *any* kind of progressive:

- Jim Webb (D, VA) is pro-gun;

- Jon Tester (D, MT) is pro-gun and pro-Drug War;

- Bob Casey (D, PA) is pro-gun; pro-life; pro-death penalty; pro-Patriot Act; and more!

Sen. Casey, in particular, ran his campaign clearly in the populist center politically—no one during the campaign would have described him as a progressive, and certainly no one looking at his voting record afterwards would! So what could Kuttner possibly mean? Well, look at the list above, and all are social issues—ones that matter to progressives. All six of the new Senators toe the line on the Democratic view of economic issues—ones that matter to liberals.

It's ok that Kuttner is a liberal. But he pretends to be a progressive. And he adds confusion to the debate between progressives and liberals, the ongoing central debate of the Democratic Party. Readers need to be careful in this book to interpret Kuttner's use of the term "progressive" because he often means "liberal." His other analysis might be interesting; but his opinions on progressivism are just factually erroneous.

Book review written Jan. 2011;
full excerpts available online at:
www.ontheissues.org/Obama_Challenge.htm

Paul vs. Obama on VoteMatch

VoteMatch is our 20-question quiz which summarizes the candidate's views on the controversial issues of the day.

VoteMatch Social Issues

	Paul	Obama
Abortion is a woman's right	opposes	strongly favors
Require companies to hire more women & minorities	strongly opposes	strongly favors
Same-sex domestic partnership benefits	favors	favors
Teacher-led prayer in public schools	favors	opposes
Parents choose schools via vouchers	favors	favors

VoteMatch Domestic Issues

	Paul	Obama
More federal funding for health coverage	opposes	strongly favors
Death Penalty	strongly opposes	opposes
Mandatory Three Strikes sentencing laws	opposes	opposes
Absolute right to gun ownership	favors	opposes
Drug use is immoral: enforce laws against it	strongly opposes	opposes

VoteMatch Economic Issues

	Paul	Obama
Privatize Social Security	strongly favors	strongly opposes
Make taxes more progressive	strongly opposes	strongly favors
Stricter limits on political campaign funds	opposes	strongly favors
Allow churches to provide welfare services	favors	favors
Replace coal & oil with alternatives	strongly opposes	strongly favors

VoteMatch International Issues

	Paul	Obama
Illegal immigrants earn citizenship	strongly opposes	favors
Support & expand free trade	opposes	opposes
The Patriot Act harms civil liberties	strongly favors	strongly favors
Expand the armed forces	opposes	favors
US out of Iraq & Afghanistan	strongly favors	favors

In our online quiz, you fill in your answers for these 20 questions, and we match you against all the candidates. Please see:

http://quiz.ontheissues.org/

Afterword

We hope that this book encourages you, as voters, to make your decisions based on the issues. We recognize the reality of American politics: voters make their decisions based primarily on whether they like the candidates. Accordingly, our goal is to get voters to compare their issue preferences in comparison to candidate issue stances when considering which candidates to like.

We intentionally omitted from this book any biographical background on Rep. Paul and President Obama. Details of their birthplaces and religious affiliations—and minutiae of every other personal detail—are readily available in the mainstream media. Their issue stances are more challenging for voters to find.

Why does the mainstream media fail at this important function? Because they are "news" organizations which are poorly suited to covering political campaigns. "News" implies reporting on what is "new": Obama's stance on criminal sentencing has not changed since 1998, and Paul's stance on the Gold standard has not changed since 1981, so there's nothing in the news about those issues. But if you are impassioned about Three Strikes, or if you vote based on Fed policy, then you cannot rely on the news media for those non-newsworthy issues. And that's where we come in.

This book represents an archive of where these two candidates stand on the key issues of our time. We don't consider whether candidates' issue stances are new—just what they say on each issue. That often requires a lot of digging on our part—we have a team of researchers to do that, but we invite you to volunteer any issue stances that we don't cover.

Our online website www.ontheissues.org covers many more issues than can fit in any book: many more stances from Barack Obama and Ron Paul, as well as all of the other 2012 candidates, Governors, Senators, and House members. We score each candidate on a 20-question quiz called "VoteMatch." A representation of the VoteMatch quiz results for the presidential contenders appears on the back cover of this book. The mainstream media interpret candidates using a one-dimensional "right-left" analysis. That simplistic analysis comes to nonsensical conclusions like calling Ron Paul "extreme right-wing" even though he opposes the Iraq War; opposes the PATRIOT Act; supports drug legalization; and supports same-sex domestic partnership benefits.

We find our two-dimensional analysis to be more accurate in differentiating candidates than that traditional one-dimensional analysis. We don't claim that our method is perfect—just superior to the simplistic mainstream media. VoteMatch uses a Social Issues dimension plus an Economic Issues dimension; we interpret candidates based on whether they believe in government involvement in either or both of those dimensions. Using the two-dimensional analysis differentiates five classes of political beliefs:

1. *Libertarian:*
   No government involvement in social issues
   No government involvement in economic issues

2. *Conservative:*
   Government involvement in social issues
   No government involvement in economic issues

3. *Liberal:*
   No government involvement in social issues
   Government involvement in economic issues

4. *Populist:*
   Government involvement in social issues
   Government involvement in economic issues

5. *Centrist:*
   Some government involvement in social issues
   Some government involvement in economic issues

Most importantly, you can answer the same 20 questions and see *your* political label and how the candidates match up with *you*. We invite you to try the VoteMatch quiz at:

http://quiz.ontheissues.org

Other Books in This Series

About the Author

Jesse Gordon has been the editor-in-chief of OnTheIssues.org since its formation in 1999. His passion revolves around providing issue-based coverage on political races, to combat the mainstream media's growing lack of such coverage.

Mr. Gordon holds a Master's degree in Public Policy from Harvard University's Kennedy School of Government. He and the website OnTheIssues.org are based in Cambridge, Massachusetts. He resides with his fiancée, Kathleen; his son Julien; Kathleen's son Derek; their cat Chanel; and six fish with whom Chanel is obsessed.

Mr. Gordon replies to email personally, at jesse@ontheissues. org—whether to suggest improvements to the website or to order one of the other books above.

www.ingramcontent.com/pod-product-compliance
Lightning Source LLC
Chambersburg PA
CBHW061259280526
45784CB00002B/819